# OFF THE BUS, INTO A SUPERCAR!

*How I became a top TV star and celebrated investor*

From the Star of the Dragons' Den

## BAYBARS ALTUNTAS

BALBOA
PRESS

A DIVISION OF HAY HOUSE

Balboa Press books may be ordered through booksellers or by contacting:

Balboa Press
A Division of Hay House
1663 Liberty Drive
Bloomington, IN 47403
www.balboapress.com
1 (877) 407-4847

Because of the dynamic nature of the Internet, any web addresses or
links contained in this book may have changed since publication and
may no longer be valid. The views expressed in this work are solely those
of the author and do not necessarily reflect the views of the publisher,
and the publisher hereby disclaims any responsibility for them.

The author of this book does not dispense medical advice or prescribe the use
of any technique as a form of treatment for physical, emotional, or medical
problems without the advice of a physician, either directly or indirectly. The
intent of the author is only to offer information of a general nature to help you
in your quest for emotional and spiritual well-being. In the event you use any
of the information in this book for yourself, which is your constitutional right,
the author and the publisher assume no responsibility for your actions.

Any people depicted in stock imagery provided by Thinkstock are models,
and such images are being used for illustrative purposes only.
Certain stock imagery © Thinkstock.

Back cover photo:
Pete Souza, The White House – Washington DC, 26th of April, 2010

Printed in the United States of America.

ISBN: 978-1-4525-2241-8 (sc)
ISBN: 978-1-4525-2240-1 (hc)
ISBN: 978-1-4525-2242-5 (e)

Balboa Press rev. date: 11/19/2014

I would like to thank all global business leaders, country leaders, policymakers, authors, Dragons of Dragons' Den, academicians, international journalists, entrepreneurs and angel investors who read my book before it was published and shared their objective and very valuable comments. I am not just thanking them for sharing their comments but also for their priceless contribution to the development of the world entrepreneurship ecosystem, for their efforts to create an awareness of entrepreneurship, for jobs they created, for their strong belief in the fact that the only way to create social justice is to support entrepreneurship, and for their unending efforts to care about a better world for the new generations.

All of us are under one umbrella:

**Entrepreneurship**

## *Global Business Leaders*

**Antony Clarke,** *Emeritus President of EBAN;* **Candace Johnson,** *President of EBAN;* **David S. Rose,** *Founder & CEO of Gust;* **Dimitris G.E. Tsigos,** *President of European Confederation of Young Entrepreneurs and Founders;* **Fadi Ghandour,** *Founder & Vice Chairman of Aramex;* **Inderjit Singh,** *Co-President of World Entrepreneurship Forum;* **John May,** *Chair Emeritus of Angel Capital Association;* **Jonathan Ortmans,** *President of Global Entrepreneurship Week;* **Muhtar Kent,** *Chairman & CEO of The Coca Cola Company;* **Paulo Andrez,** *Emeritus President of EBAN,* **Plamen Russev,** *President of Webit Congress;* **Temel Kotil,** *President of Turkish Airlines;* **Prof Tugrul Atamer,** *Executive Chairman of World Entrepreneurship Forum;* **Yousef M. Hamidaddin,** *CEO of Oasis500*

# Country Leaders

**Albert Colomer,** *President, Business Angels Network of Catalunya (BANC);* **Alejtin Berisha,** *President, Kosovo Business Angels Network (KOBAN);* **Aleksandar Cabrilo,** *President, Serbian Business Angels Network (SBAN);* **Francisco Banha,** *President, Portuguese Federation of Business Angels Associations (FNABA);* **Hasan Haider,** *Founder and CEO, the Bahraini Business Angels Organization (TENMOU);* **Ivar Siimar,** *President, Estonian Business Angels Network (EstBAN);* **Jesper Jarlbaek,** *President, Business Angels Copenhagen (BAC);* **Juan Roure,** *President, Spanish Federation of Business Angels Network (AEBAN);* **Konstantin Fokin,** *President, National Business Angels Association of Russia (NBAAR);* **Manhong Mannie Liu,** *Founder and honorary Chair, China Business Angel Association (CBAA);* **Padmaja Ruparel,** *President, Indian Angel Network (IAN);* **Riku Asikainen,** *President, Finnish Business Angels Network (FBAN);* **Selma Prodanovic,** *Co-founder and CEO, Austrian Angel Investors Association (AAIA)*

# Authors

**Dave Berkus,** *Berkonomics;* **David Drake,** *The SPPICE of Crowdfunding;* **David S. Rose,** *Angel Investing: The Gust Guide to Making Money & Having Fun Investing in Startups;* **Inderjit Singh,** *The Art and Science of Entrepreneurship;* **John May,** *Every Business Needs an Angel;* **Marius Ghenea,** *Entrepreneurship;* **Melinda Emerson,** *Become Your Own Boss in 12 months;* **Mirela Sula,** *Don't Let Your Mind Go;* **Modwenna Rees-Mogg,** *The Unofficial Guide to Dragons' Den: Dragons or Angels;* **Dr Nikhil Agarwal,** *Planet Entrepreneur;* **Plamen Russev,** *Power to the People;* **Selma Pradonovic,** *Brainsbook on Networking;* **Steven D. Strauss,** *The Small Business Bible*

# Dragons of Dragons' Den

Gamze Cizreli, *Turkey,* Marek Rusiecki, *Poland;* Marius
Ghenea, *Romania;* Riku Asikainen, *Finland;* Sean
O'Sullivan, *Ireland;* Selma Pradonovic, *Austria*

# Policy Makers

**Their Royal Highnesses;**
**Crown Prince Alexander and Crown Princess Katherine**
*Royal Palace, Belgrade*
**Inderjit Singh**
*Member of Parliament, Government of Singapore*
**Ali Arslan**
*General Director, Directorate of Financial Sector
Relations and Exchange, Government of Turkey*

# Academicians

**Alejtin Berish,** *President of Universum College;* **Prof Aysegul
Toker,** *Dean of Faculty of Economics and Administrative
Sciences, Bogazici University;* **Francisco Banha,** *Professor of
MBA Programmes, The Technical University of Lisbon;* **Hedda
Pahlson-Moller,** *Professor of Business Policy and Strategy,
European University of Luxembourg;* **Juan Roure,** *Professor of
Entrepreneurship, IESE Business School;* **Prof Manhong Mannie
Liu,** *Professor of Entrepreneurship & Innovation Renmin University;*
**Raomal Perera,** *Professor of Entrepreneurship INSEAD;* **Prof
Tugrul Atamer,** *Vice President of Emlyon Business School*

# International Journalists

**Amal Daraghmeh Masri,** *Middle East Business News & Magazine;*
**David Drake,** *Forbes Magazine, Entrepreneur.com, Huffington Post;*
**Melinda Emerson,** *SmallBizLady;* **Mirela Sula,** *Migrant Woman;*
**Modwenna Rees-Mogg,** *AngelNews,* **Steven D. Strauss,** *USA Today*

# Entrepreneurs & Angel Investors

**Dr Abdul Malik Al Jaber,** *United Arab Emirates;* **Albert Colomer,**
*Catalunya;* **Alejtin Berisha,** *Kosovo;* **Aleksandar Cabrilo,** *Serbia;*
**Aleksandar Tasev,** *Macedonia;* **Amal Daraghmeh Masri,** *Palastine;*
**Anthony Clarke,** *UK;* **Ari Korhonen,** *Finland;* **Candace Johnson,**
*France;* **Dave Berkus,** *USA,* **David Drake,** *USA;* **David S. Rose,**
*USA;* **David Thomas,** *Autralia;* **Dimitris G.E. Tsigos,** *Greece;*
**Fadi Ghandour,** *Jordan;* **Francisco Banha,** *Portugal;* **G.Antonio**
**Sosa-Pascual,** *Puerto Rico;* **Gamze Cizreli,** *Turkey;* **Hasan**
**Haider,** *Bahrain;* **Hedda Pahlson-Moller,** *Luxembourg;* **Inderjit**
**Singh,** *Singapore;* **Ivar Siimar,** *Estonia;* **Jeanette Andersson,**
*Sweden;* **Jesper Jarlbaek,** *Denmark;* **John May,** *USA;* **Jonathan**
**Ortmans,** *USA;* **Juan Roure,** *Spain;* **Konstantin Fokin,** *Russia;*
**Prof Manhong Mannie Liu,** *China;* **Marek Rusiecki,** *Poland;*
**Marius Ghenea,** *Romania;* **Melinda Emerson,** *USA;* **Mirela Sula,**
*Albania;* **Modwenna Rees-Mogg,** *UK;* **Dr Nikhil Agarwal,** *UK;*
**Padmaja Ruparel,** *India;* **Paulo Andrez,** *Portugal;* **Peter E. Braun,**
*Switzerland;***Plamen Russev,** *Bulgaria;* **Raomal Perera,** *France;*
**Ricardo Luz,** *Portugal;* **Riku Asikainen,** *Finland;* **Sean O'Sullivan,**
*Ireland;* **Selma Prodanovic,** *Austria;* **Steven D. Strauss,** *USA;*
**William Stevens,** *Belgium;* **Yousef M. Hamidaddin,** *Jordan*

*"We would like to thank to Baybars Altuntas for his great contribution to the global entrepreneurship ecosystem by writing this book. He outlines very practical ideas for would-be entrepreneurs aiming to set up their own businesses, and for entrepreneurs who are growing their businesses."*

**Their Royal Highnesses**
*Crown Prince Alexander and Crown Princess Katherine*
*Royal Palace, Belgrade*

"The most important global challenge of the 21$^{st}$ century is creating new jobs for new generations. IT and mobile technology investments are increasing globally, which results in fewer people being recruited for new jobs. Because technology handles so much of the work, there will be less demand for manpower. The only solution to this challenge is to create a different mindset for the young generation. This new mindset is very clear: Set up your own business instead of looking for a job!

We would like to thank to Baybars Altuntas for his great contribution to the global entrepreneurship ecosystem by writing this book. He outlines very practical ideas for would-be entrepreneurs aiming to set up their own businesses, and for entrepreneurs who are growing their businesses. Creating wealth, jobs and social justice are three key concepts of entrepreneurship. This book shows how these can make a real impact on society when they are taken seriously by astute entrepreneurs like Baybars.

This book should be required reading for anyone studying entrepreneurship at university, particularly those students who are aspiring to start their own businesses. Entrepreneurship is the backbone of every successful market economy. Having confidence in oneself is key to successful entrepreneurship. Nothing is impossible."

*"In his book Altuntas tells the story of a dynamic and energetic entrepreneur. In his exciting journey, he masterfully takes you through pitfalls and challenges, as well as opportunities and intelligent risk-taking, all of which cumulate into important learning events."*

*Muhtar Kent, USA*
*Chairman and CEO*
*The Coca-Cola Company*

"In his book Altuntas tells the story of a dynamic and energetic entrepreneur. In his exciting journey, he masterfully takes you through pitfalls and challenges, as well as opportunities and intelligent risk-taking, all of which cumulate into important learning events. As you progress through the book, you feel the passion, courage and dedication from cover to cover."

*"I encourage all who want to embark on the entrepreneurial road to read the book and to learn from Baybars' experience."*

*Inderjit Singh, Singapore*
*Member of Parliament, Government of Singapore*
*Co-President, World Entrepreneurship Forum*
*Author of The Art and Science of Entrepreneurship*

"Entrepreneurs face challenges no matter in which part of the world they start their companies. Every successful entrepreneur will tell you that the first step of the journey is transforming the mindset so that one that believes all problems can be solved. In this book, Baybars shares his journey and tells how he succeeded as an entrepreneur and

I encourage all who want to embark on the entrepreneurial road to read the book and to learn from Baybars' experience."

## "This book is one of the world's top 5 titles on entrepreneurship and startups."

*Prof. Tugrul Atamer, France*
*Executive Chairman, World Entrepreneurship Forum*
*Vice President, Emlyon Business School*

"I picked up the original Turkish version of this book from the bestseller shelf in the bookstore at the Istanbul airport while waiting for a flight to Lyon. Arriving in Lyon 4 hours later, I had finished the book, all in a single sitting.

Baybars Altuntas shares the secrets of becoming a successful entrepreneur in this light-hearted account of his own journey. He lays out a practical roadmap that can easily be followed by anyone, no matter who or where they are. His concept of "rising steps" is brilliant: wannapreneurship, innovation, entrepreneurship, marketing and sales, branding, institutionalization, franchising, leadership and angel investment. He takes you by the hand, describing in clear detail each step of the way. As you progress, you also learn about various ways to access financing, from bootstrapping, to angel investors, to VCs and banks.

Baybars sagely advises us, however, that networking is far more important than finance. He provides real examples from his own life story and you come to the realization that, if you can manage to actualize the Altuntas principle of converting idle capacity into cash, then you've made it, You will have become a successful entrepreneur without any financing at all!

As the Executive Chairman of the World Entrepreneurship Forum, I follow closely the latest publications on entrepreneurship. I rank this book as one of the world's top 5 titles on entrepreneurship and start-ups. Not only is it informative, it's a delightful read as well. Highly recommended for young entrepreneurs wanting to set up their own businesses and for others aiming to grow theirs."

*"A rollicking, inspirational and highly personal journey through the life of a self-made business executive who has dedicated much of his career to bringing entrepreneurship to the Near and Middle East."*

*David S. Rose, USA*
*Founder, New York Angels; CEO of Gust*
*Author of the New York Times bestseller*
*Angel Investing: The Gust Guide to Making Money*
*& Having Fun Investing in Startups*

"Baybars Altuntaş is an entrepreneurial ball of fire who has almost singlehandedly put Turkey on the global map of innovation centers. His book, *Off the Bus, Into a Supercar!* is a rollicking, inspirational and highly personal journey through the life of a self-made business executive who has dedicated much of his career to bringing entrepreneurship to the Near and Middle East. The lessons he has learned—and that he now teaches through this spirited, optimistic autobiography—are ones that every aspiring entrepreneur should heed!"

*"An interesting entrepreneurial story full of anecdotes and lessons with lots of passion."*

*Fadi Ghandour, Jordan*
*Founder & Vice Chairman*
*Aramex*

"Entrepreneurship is at the core of addressing the future challenges of societies, whether advanced or in the process of developing. It is a process that should be embraced and nurtured by every society. Altuntas tells us an interesting entrepreneurial story full of anecdotes and lessons with lots of passion. It is enjoyable and easy to read. Check it out."

*"Baybars is just this sort of person. In the pages of this book, you will read the fascinating story of his road to success. He is truly an inspiration for everyone."*

**Dr Temel Kotil, Turkey**
*Chief Executive Officer, President and General Manager*
*Turkish Airlines*

"Success can be defined in many ways. No matter how you conceptualize and define it, success derives from a capacity to make the most of opportunities that present themselves and the ability to use these in a way that benefits humanity.

Even a single individual can produce important things for humanity. He may write a story that will be appreciated by the future generations, for example. If a person with a story can look forward to the future, he can pair his optimism with entrepreneurship. This sort of person is always ready for something new and can therefore be productive. People who never lose hope will enjoy life more than those who do. The will to grasp onto life without losing hope brings love, and this love brings success.

Baybars is just this sort of person. In the pages of this book, you will read the fascinating story of his road to success. He is truly an inspiration for everyone."

*'His book relates in no small detail each step of his journey."*

**Candace Johnson, France**
*President, European Business Angels Network*

"Baybars Altuntas has had a remarkable personal journey from small businessman to entrepreneur to business angel. His book relates in no small detail each step of his journey. It is a fascinating account of one man's story from rags to riches and how he has helped others achieve their goals as well."

**"Baybars' life story proves it can be done."**

**Anthony Clarke, UK**
*Founder and CEO, Angel Capital Group*
*President Emeritus of European Business Angels Association*

"Successful entrepreneurs need not only passion, enthusiasm and belief; they also need courage to turn their dreams into reality. Baybars' life story proves it can be done and should encourage others like him to follow their dreams."

**"This book is a must for all those who dream and have the will to succeed!"**

**Paulo Andrez, Portugal**
*President Emeritus, EBAN, European Trade*
*Association for Business Angels*
*and Early Stage Market Players*

"Many people tell me they have a dream of creating a company, but they do not have resources, they do not have time, they do not have a good idea, they do not...they do not... Baybars shows in this book that any person with the right mindset can create a successful business even if they lack resources. What they need is the most powerful tool—the will to succeed. This book is a must for all those who dream and have the will to succeed!"

## "Aspiring young entrepreneurs, you will enjoy this book!"

**John May, USA**
*Chair Emeritus, Angel Capital Association*
*Co-author of Every Business Needs an Angel*

*"Off the Bus, Into a Supercar!* is more than a personal success story of one entrepreneur's accomplishment of driving himself along life's highway. It is a roadmap for others to follow as they too try to escape bureaucracy and big company environment and create his or her own enterprise from their own vision. I have watched Baybars grow and blossom over the last decade and look forward to many great things from his energy and passion, Aspiring young entrepreneurs, you will enjoy this book!"

## "An absolute must-read for anyone who wants to discover the Holy Grail of entrepreneurship"

**Dimitris G.E. Tsigos, Greece**
*President, European Confederation of Young*
*Entrepreneurs and Founders*
*(YES for Europe)*
*CEO, StartTech Ventures*

"One of the best basketball players of all times, Earvin "Magic" Johnson, once remarked that "neither the tallest nor the strongest players gets the rebound, but the one who wants it most". While this inspiring quote is certainly true for basketball, it is probably even more relevant for entrepreneurship. It's all about determination and all the rest will follow. Baybars Altuntas serves as an outstanding example of what strong will and determination can achieve, even in the most challenging situations. His exciting book *Off the Bus, Into a Supercar!* is an absolute must read for anyone who wants to discover the Holy Grail of entrepreneurship, which is the unparalleled happiness of managing to be creative and useful at the same time."

*"Anyone who is planning to set up their own business should definitely read this book first!"*

*Plamen Russev, Bulgaria*
*Founder & Chairman, Webit Global Congress*
*Author of Power to the People*

"I meet frequently with some of the world's most distinguished leaders in entrepreneurship, innovation and angel investment. Baybars is one of the most inspirational role models for entrepreneurs and would-be-entrepreneurs that I've ever met. His drive and enthusiasm for for business and for life in general is reflected in this engaging story about how he capitalized on his natural talents to develop into a world-class dynamo in the world of entrepreneurship. Anyone who is planning to set up their own business should definitely read this book first!"

*"I've written and read numerous books on entrepreneurism. This is one of the very best."*

*Dave Berkus, USA*
*Chairman Emeritus, Tech Coast Angels*
*Creator of Berkonomics*
*Author of Berconomics*

"I just finished reading this book - and am a Baybars Altuntas fan for life. Altuntas tells wonderful stories about entrepreneurs, his history as an entrepreneur, and gives priceless advice to others. He invites us to become wise entrepreneurs, to follow his simple steps in preparation, cautions us about pitfalls, and encourages us to take an appropriate amount of risk. You'll smile, even laugh at his stories of success and failure as each teaches a lesson about entrepreneurism. I've written and read numerous books on entrepreneurism. This is one of the very best.!!"

### *"A book I will add to the reading list that all our founders need to study."*

*Yousef M. Hamidaddin, Jordan*
*Chief Executive Officer, Oasis 500*

"What a read! At Oasis 500 our focus is on investing in ideas, working with founders, and supporting start-ups. Baybars is an inspiration for all, and his is a book I will add to the reading list that all our founders need to study. Baybars is a story close to home, easy to relate to and therefore inspiring for entrepreneurs across MENA. We need more Baybars."

### *"When you read this book, you will understand that entrepreneurship is not constrained by age or background. Even university students can create a multi-million dollar business from scratch if they have the right mindset."*

*Prof. Ayse Gul Toker, Turkey*
*Dean, Faculty of Economics and Administrative Sciences*
*Bogazici University*

"The academic and social environment at Bogazici University, together with its unique culture, nurture creativity and encourage young minds to start their own business while they are still students.

Baybars, a graduate of our university, has become a key player in the entrepreneurship ecosystem both in Turkey and the global arena, and we are extremely proud of his accomplishments.

When you read this book, you will understand that entrepreneurship is not constrained by age or background. Even university students can create a multi-million-dollar business from scratch if they have the right mindset. Baybars' book is on the reading list for our entrepreneurship classes, as it provides valuable practical advice on setting up and running a successful business. Highly recommended."

### *"This book is full of these abrupt realizations that highlight when the emperor has no clothes..."*

*Sean O'Sullivan, Ireland*
*Founder and CEO, SOS Ventures*
*Chair, Irish Entrepreneurship Forum*
*TV Star, Dragon of Dragons' Den*

"An entertaining tale of a hard-scrabble yet joyful man rising up through his own grit and non-stop opportunity seizing to become an enabler to presidents and prime ministers and an inspirational leader and networker to the entrepreneurs and would-be entrepreneurs everywhere.

Baybars is an amazing man, a friendly and fearless, gutsy and driven person. Having met him on a number of occasions at a variety of entrepreneurial and angel events, I can attest that positivity and possibilities flow from him ceaselessly. The materials cover his remarkable life experience with franchising, education, tourism and angel investing.

Hard-hitting and sensible advice for those seeking angel investment. Pithy bits of wisdom like "first sell, then spend" help separate the wheat from the chaff, and this book is full of these abrupt realizations that highlight when the emperor has no clothes... and help give entrepreneurs their grounding while simultaneously helping them reach for the sky."

*"If you want to get into your own supercar, this is the book for you!"*

**Steven D. Strauss, USA**
*USA TODAY Senior Small Business Columnist*
*Author of The Small Business Bible*

"I have met many entrepreneurs over the years, but Baybars Altuntas may be my favorite, and this great book will show you why. In it, you will find not only tried-and-true, real life, smart strategies for how you too can become a successful entrepreneur, but his infectious optimism will help guide you along the journey. If you want to get into your own supercar, this is the book for you!"

*"He teaches you different ways of thinking, gives bright ideas and hints, and helps you change your mindset in order to succeed in business."*

**Gamze Cizreli, Turkey**
*Founder and CEO, BigChefs Restaurants Franchise Chain*
*Awarded the Best Woman Entrepreneur of Turkey*
*TV Star, Dragon of Dragons' Den*

"Beyond being an entrepreneur sitting next to me on Dragons' Den, Baybars is also a talented teacher for young entrepreneurs. Anyone wanting to become an entrepreneur should certainly read this book and benefit from his experience. He teaches you different ways of thinking, gives bright ideas and hints, and helps you change your mindset in order to succeed in business. Most importantly, he encourages you not to give up but to solve the problems you face. There is no other guide demonstrating entrepreneurship so clearly."

*"I highly recommend this enjoyable book for entrepreneurs all over the world."*

**Melinda Emerson, USA**
*"SmallBizLady"*
*Forbes #1 Influential Woman for Entrepreneurs*
*Author of the bestseller Become Your Own Boss in 12 months*

"*Off the Bus, into a Supercar!* is a wonderful resource for entrepreneurs, providing clues on financing a new business or startup and ways to run and grow the business. I love how Baybars teaches his unique strategy, the Altuntas Principle: how to convert idle capacity into cash. He gives you the secrets of how you too can succeed, even without financing. I highly recommend this enjoyable book to entrepreneurs all over the world.'

*"One of the most honest, refreshing, entertaining and enjoyable business books I have read."*

**Modwenna Rees-Mogg, UK**
*Co-founder, UK Business Angels Institute*
*Founder and CEO, AngelNews*
*Author of The Unofficial Guide to Dragons' Den: Dragons or Angels*

"Stop! Pick up this book! Sit down and read in one gulp! *Off the Bus, Into a Supercar!* is one of the most honest, refreshing, entertaining and enjoyable business books I have read. Baybars Altuntas is not just a great entrepreneur he is also a great writer. You will gallop though the story of his entrepreneurial life, his pearls of wisdom on setting up a successful business and on how to be an investor who backs the right entrepreneurs, not the wrong ones."

*"If you want to become an entrepreneur, read this book. If you are already an entrepreneur, read it. If you ever have a chance to meet with Baybars Altuntas in person, take it."*

*Peter E. Braun, Switzerland*
*Serial Entrepreneur & Angel Investor*

"This book is about bravery. It is about belief. It is about a great personality. It is about one of the greatest entrepreneurs I know. A true self-made man who took his life into his own hands, against all odds. Baybars shares stories from his childhood with us (read how he made his first dollar in fourth grade – it's fun) until his more recent successes and greatest achievements. His vita is truly striking. I have the pleasure of serving with him on the board of directors of EBAN and he is one of the nicest people I know: inspiring, brilliantly witty, creative and fully dedicated to entrepreneurship. If you want to become an entrepreneur, read this book. If you are already an entrepreneur, read it. If you ever have a chance to meet with Baybars Altuntas in person, take it."

*"I strongly recommend this book for entrepreneurs, particularly for those at the beginning of their careers."*

**Ali Arslan, Turkey**
*General Director*
*General Directorate of Financial Sector Relations and Exchange*
*Government of Turkey*

"Baybars Altuntas is not only a successful entrepreneur but also an influential writer. *Off the Bus, Into a Supercar!* will help expand your horizons as a tool to think outside the box and increase the capacity to dream. Mr. Altuntas encourages entrepreneurs and gives significant insight and useful information on how to turn their dreams into a profitable future. The most striking part of the book is the experience lived by the author himself. I strongly recommend this book for all entrepreneurs, particularly those at the beginning of their careers."

*"This is a must for anyone thinking of starting their own business."*

**Raomal Perera, France**
*Adjunct Professor of Entrepreneurship INSEAD*
*One of the 40 entrepreneurs worldwide chosen as a*
*Technology Pioneer of the World Economic Forum (WEF)*

"This is a must for anyone thinking of starting their own business but who has doubts and fears. Baybars from Turkey talks about his journey, which will amaze you. It is a very easy and pleasurable read and I thoroughly enjoyed it. Thank you, Baybars."

*"He shares his experiences and lessons learned with everyone who wants to be successful."*

**Prof. Manhong Mannie Liu, China**
*Professor of Entrepreneurship and Innovation, Renmin University*
*Director, Venture Capital Research Group at the Chinese Academy*
*of Science, Center for Fictitious Economy and Data Research*
*Founder and Honorary Chair of the China Business Angel Association*

"I met my friend Baybars at an international business angel investment event. I was extremely impressed with his enthusiasm, his energy, his commitment and his vibrant personality. Style is the man. His book *Off the Bus, Into a Supercar!* is his own life story. It is an incredible account of how a person with no money and no background in business became a successful entrepreneur. What impressed me most is that Baybars has a big heart. He shares his experiences and lessons learned with everyone who wants to be successful. That's the Baybars Altuntas I know."

*'"He is an amazing inspirational role model who gives people around the world a genuine lesson in optimism."*

**Dr Abdul Malik Al Jaber, United Arab Emirates**
*Founder and Chairman, Arabreneur*

"When I'm speaking to young people, specially those from less privileged communities, I tell them "where you start your life may not be up to you, but where you end is in your hands, and no one can stop you". I have seen this with Baybars. He is an amazing inspirational role model who gives people around the world a genuine lesson in optimism, positive thinking, determination and having faith in your capability to achieve your goals."

*"Baybars is an inspiration to entrepreneurs all over the world."*

**David Thomas, Australia**
*Vice President, Australia China Business Council*
*BRIC Expert; Thought Leader*

"Baybars is an inspiration to entrepreneurs all over the world, and particularly in Turkey. Spending a day with Baybars in Istanbul you start to understand his popularity and celebrity status as an Angel Investor and Chief Dragon. Young budding entrepreneurs approach him on the street asking him to sprinkle magic dust on their ideas and encouragement to pursue their dreams. In a new age of entrepreneurialism, innovation and SMEs, the experience, wisdom and courage of people like Baybars will be essential to power the global economy."

*"The Tool for Entrepreneurs section is a very practical guide for would-be-entrepreneurs."*

**Padmaja Ruparel, India**
*President, Indian Angel Network*

"Baybars' journey of entrepreneurship is a dream come true – and very inspirational. But even more importantly, in this book he proves that entrepreneurship is life-changing and changes lives – in Turkey and beyond! The Tool for Entrepreneurs section is a very practical guide for would-be-entrepreneurs."

*"It is one of the rare books that will have you hooked from the first page."*

*Alejtin Berisha, Kosovo*
*President, Universum College*
*President, Kosovo Business Angels Network*

"*Off the Bus, Into a Supercar!* is an inspirational, informative and compelling book for all future entrepreneurs. A truly remarkable story by one of Turkey's most distinguished entrepreneurs, *Off the Bus, Into a Supercar!* shows you the determination, passion and skills required to excel in today's business world. It is one of the rare books that will have you hooked from the first page, while making sure that you will also learn some of the most important skills in becoming a successful entrepreneur in sales, negotiation and problem solving. A must read!"

*"After reading his book, I said "Yes, I can achieve it!"*

*Mirela Sula, Albania*
*Co-founder & Editor-in-Chief, UK's Migrant Woman magazine*
*Leader of the Women's Network: Equality in Decision Making*
*Author of Don't Let Your Mind Go*

"I read the Albanian translation of this book while flying to London from Tirana. In his book Baybars Altuntas shows us the right road to follow. He knows the road well because he has been there, and this book proves he is an excellent driver. He drove himself towards great success, abundance, peace, love and happiness. Isn't this all that we want in life? He achieved these and believes that we can do it as well. His stories and wisdom are not only inspiring but also healing and stimulating. After reading his book, I said "Yes, I can achieve it!"

## "It is one of the rare books that will have you hooked from the first page."

*Alejtin Berisha, Kosovo*
*President, Universum College*
*President, Kosovo Business Angels Network*

"*Off the Bus, Into a Supercar!* is an inspirational, informative and compelling book for all future entrepreneurs. A truly remarkable story by one of Turkey's most distinguished entrepreneurs, *Off the Bus, Into a Supercar!* shows you the determination, passion and skills required to excel in today's business world. It is one of the rare books that will have you hooked from the first page, while making sure that you will also learn some of the most important skills in becoming a successful entrepreneur in sales, negotiation and problem solving. A must read!"

## "After reading his book, I said "Yes, I can achieve it!"

*Mirela Sula, Albania*
*Co-founder & Editor-in-Chief, UK's Migrant Woman magazine*
*Leader of the Women's Network: Equality in Decision Making*
*Author of Don't Let Your Mind Go*

"I read the Albanian translation of this book while flying to London from Tirana. In his book Baybars Altuntas shows us the right road to follow. He knows the road well because he has been there, and this book proves he is an excellent driver. He drove himself towards great success, abundance, peace, love and happiness. Isn't this all that we want in life? He achieved these and believes that we can do it as well. His stories and wisdom are not only inspiring but also healing and stimulating. After reading his book, I said "Yes, I can achieve it!"

*"If you want to taste this cocktail of entrepreneurship and innovation, you will enjoy this book very much."*

**Albert Colomer, Catalunya**
*President, Business Angels Network of Catalunya (BANC)*

"Just a taste of this cocktail: the vision of an innovator, the soul of an entrepreneur, the wings of a business angel, the world knowledge of this hearty man, mixed in the correct proportions, served in the Baybars style of living. All these demonstrate, for all to see, the power of determination. If you want to taste this cocktail of entrepreneurship and innovation, you will enjoy this book very much."

*"His new book is not the usual easily forgotten story but instead, an honest, thoughtful and (even more importantly) an action-provoking testimonial."*

**Konstantin Fokin, Russia**
*President, National Business Angels Association of Russia*
*CEO, Centre for Innovation Development of the City of Moscow*

"Baybars is a serious, 100% passionate doer, the man you can always rely on, a real entrepreneur and risk-taker. His new book is not the usual easily forgotten story but instead, an honest, thoughtful and (even more importantly) an action-provoking testimonial. His experience, his ups and downs, his successes and failures, accompanied by boiling adrenalin will no doubt inspire many young people to do more - think big, work hard, build teams, make their dreams come true. I am sure of this. He did it, and so can you!"

*"I can guarantee you will be thrilled, intrigued and inspired."*

**Dr. Nikhil Agarwal, UK**
*President, Cambridge Global Partners (CGP)*
*Co-founder, QuestionBox.org*
*Co-author of Planet Entrepreneur*

"Baybars' book on entrepreneurship is just not any ordinary book. It is a hobbit-style adventure and experience of a lifetime. I can guarantee you will be thrilled, intrigued and inspired. A must read for everybody. I can't wait for another book from Baybars."

*"The American dream is possible everywhere if you really believe in yourself and work hard."*

**Aleksandar Cabrilo, Serbia**
*President, Serbian Business Angels Network (SBAN)*
*CEO, High Tech Engineering Center*

"Baybars' example shows that the American dream is possible everywhere if you really believe in yourself and work hard. This book will motivate many young people to become entrepreneurs and shape the future. Some will also become authors who are referenced in biographies of new global leaders, having being inspired by this story."

*"This book is the true life story of a global entrepreneur and angel investor who started from scratch. You must read, study and learn from it."*

**Ricardo Luz, Portugal**
*President, Invicta Angels*
*Vice-President, Federation of Business Angels*
*Networks of Portugal (FNABA)*

"Baybars believes dreams can come true. His strong will and hard work made him a global role model for would-be entrepreneurs. Now, as a business angel he invests in people that have the same strengths, helping them to achieve their dreams. This book is the true life story of a global entrepreneur and angel investor who started from scratch. You must read, study and learn from it."

*"A must read for entrepreneurs from around the world wishing to become company presidents or one of the greatest entrepreneurs of our time."*

**Selma Prodanovic, Austria**
*Co-founder and CEO, Austrian Angel Investors Association (AAIA)*
*Author of Brainsbook on Networking*
*TV Star, Dragon of Dragons' Den*

"*Off the Bus, Into a Supercar!* shows how running a successful multi-million dollar business is no longer the privilege of the few but is a dream come true for entrepreneurs in all corners of the world. No matter how good or bad your starting position was, today you can make your own decisions, find your own way, and make it to the top. A must read for entrepreneurs from around the world wishing to become company presidents or one of the greatest entrepreneurs of our time."

*"This is a book which should be read by all entrepreneurs and angel investors!"*

*Ari Korhonen, Finland*
*Founder and CEO, Lagoon Capital*
*Vice President, European Business Angels Network*

"Baybars Altuntas is a living example of an innovative and dynamic entrepreneur who has shown that everything is possible. He is the Dragon! He met Obama! He is a celebrity! He is writing bestsellers! Baybars has demonstrated to all of us that if there is a will, there is a way. This is a book which should be read by all entrepreneurs and angel investors!"

*"Great benchmark for entrepreneurs around the world."*

*G. Antonio Sosa-Pascual, Puerto Rico*
*Managing Director, REOF Capital*
*2013's Best Talent of Puerto Rico under 40*

"Funny, practical and inspiring. The man walks on water. Great benchmark for entrepreneurs around the world. Could not stop laughing."

*"Baybars' story shows us all that there is no path in life as attractive as the choice of being an entrepreneur."*

**William Stevens, Belgium**
*CEO and Founder, Europe Unlimited*

"We are all inspired by personal stories. Baybars' success story is particularly engaging and energizing. His life is a role model for those seeking to start a business or who are already running one. Baybars' story shows us all that there is no path in life as attractive as the choice of being an entrepreneur."

*"Off the Bus, Into a Supercar! shows how to be a dragon entrepreneur in real life."*

**Aleksandar Tasev, Macedonia**
*President, SuperFounders*
*CEO, Balkan Unlimited*

"Plain and simple, *Off the Bus, Into a Supercar!* shows how to be a dragon entrepreneur in real life. The Dragons' Den star Baybars Altuntas gives us his exhilarating personal story from a humble childhood to global success, accompanied by well-thought-out advice supported by real life examples. *Off the Bus, Into a Supercar!* is not only a recipe for success, but also highly entertaining book for just about anybody, and it is a motivating read for aspiring entrepreneurs. Baybars shows through his personal example how the entrepreneurial voyage "from the bus to the supercar" can be fun and thrilling!"

## "Brilliantly done, my fellow Dragon from another country!"

**Marius Ghenea, Romania**
*Angel Investor*
*Author of Entrepreneurship*
*Tv Star, Dragon of Dragons' Den*

"*Off the Bus, Into a Supercar!* is a book that displays a unique combination of a spectacular yet very normal entrepreneurial success story with some very well structured lessons for all wannapreneurs and entrepreneurs alike. I was fascinated by the way Baybars switches back and forth between his own fascinating life story and the sound pedagogical-style advice he gives to the next generation of entrepreneurs not only of Turkey, but of the entire world. Brilliantly done, my fellow Dragon from another country!"

## "It draws you in like an adventure tale—I strongly recommend it!"

**Marek Rusiecki, Poland**
*Founder and CEO, Xevin Investments*
*TV Star, Dragon of Dragons' Den*

"This book is a total must-read for every entrepreneur, as it is a perfect example of a zero-to-hero story. Baybars has achieved it and describes his journey in an incredibly vivid way. It draws you in like an adventure tale—I strongly recommend it!"

*"Read the book and you will realize that, with conviction and persistence, anything is possible."*

**Jesper Jarlbaek, Denmark**
*President, Business Angels Copenhagen (BAC)*
*Vice President, Danish Venture Capital Association (DVCA)*
*Chairman, CataCap Private Equity; Board Member, Bang & Olufsen A/S*

"Baybars' book proves that true entreprenuership is a universal phenomenon unlimited by boundaries, cultures or age. His very entertaining life story includes a wealth of valuable advice based on personal experience. Baybars' can-do attitude took him all the way to the White House to meet President Obama. Read the book and you will realize that, with conviction and persistence, anything is possible."

*"This book will make you laugh, this book will make you think, but most importantly through his own life experience, Baybars manages to inspire those young would-be entrepreneurs whose starting platform is a dusty village road."*

**Ivar Siimar, Estonia**
*President, Estonian Business Angels Network (EstBAN)*

"Baybars has written something truly wonderful here. It is a must read for all future entrepreneurs who have not yet taken the final leap. All budding entrepreneurs need real-life success stories for inspiration and courage to help them take the first steps. We also need to accept the unavoidability of failures and learn from them. This book will make you laugh, this book will make you think, but most importantly through his own life experience, Baybars manages to inspire those young would-be entrepreneurs whose starting platform is a dusty village road."

*"His journey from very modest background to represent his country at the White House is extraordinary."*

*Riku Asikainen, Finland*
*President, Finnish Business Angels Network*
*Tv Star, Dragon of Dragons' Den*

"Baybars' story is certainly an inspiration to us all. His journey from a very modest background to represent his country at the White House is extraordinary. But that is not my major take from this business book. Rather, the most important point Baybars formulates is that of entrepreneurial spirit, for he is one of the few that can really make change, create growth and above all show prudent leadership."

*"I wish I had had this book to read when I started my business 16 years ago."*

*Amal Daraghmeh Masri, Palestine*
*Founder & Editor-in-Chief, Middle East Business News & Magazine*
*Awarded Best Woman Entrepreneur in Middle East and North Africa*

"As an entrepreneur myself, reading through Baybars' strong and firm words, I was able to appreciate how these words will shine a guiding light for future young entrepreneurs. At the start of their journey, entrepreneurs need encouraging words, and even this simple requirement is not easy to fulfill. This book addresses that need. I wish I had had it to read when I started my business 16 years ago. The words reflect the generous nature of the writer and his desire to encourage others. He shows a great spirit of willingness to connect entrepreneurs. Well done, Baybars."

*"This excellent book, which I hope can instill in students, entrepreneur candidates, entrepreneurs, and investors looking for opportunities, the necessary inspiration for the creation of new companies. And for current entrepreneurs, it can help foster the evolution of social and economic welfare."*

**Francisco Banha, Portugal**
*President, Portuguese Federation of Business Angels Associations (FNABA)*
*Co-founder and Board Member, World Business Angels Association (WBAA)*
*Professor of Entrepreneurship – MBA, the Technical University of Lisbon*

"Congratulations to Baybars for this excellent book, which I hope can instill in students, entrepreneur candidates, entrepreneurs, and investors looking for opportunities, the necessary inspiration for the creation of new companies. And for current entrepreneurs, it can help foster the evolution of social and economic welfare.

And because books are two-way paths, do not miss the opportunity to send feedback to Baybars. Email was created for this very reason."

*"A great promoter of entrepreneurship and angel investment around the world."*

**Hasan Haider, Bahrain**
*Founder and CEO, the Bahraini Business Angels Organization (TENMOU)*

"Baybars is a great promoter of entrepreneurship and angel investment around the world, and it is great to read how his own entrepreneurial story started in Turkey. I highly recommend following in the footsteps of this great connector of people."

*"Wonderful history of an outstanding entrepreneur. If you want to learn about real entrepreneurship, you must read this book."*

**Juan Roure, Spain**
*Professor of Entrepreneurship, IESE Business School*
*President of the Spanish Federation of*
*Business Angels Network (AEBAN)*

"Wonderful history of an outstanding entrepreneur. If you want to learn about real entrepreneurship, you must read this book."

*"Incredible journey of one of the key players in the European Business Angel community"*

**Jeanette Andersson, Sweden**
*Business Angels Network Manager, CONNECT*

"Baybars has played an important role in developing the European Business Angel market and improving cooperation and cross-border investments between the EU and Turkey. His energy and commitment on the EBAN board to develop the business angel market in Europe has made him one of the key players in the European business angels community. It is a great opportunity for all entrepreneurs, existing and potential, to learn about Baybars' incredible journey for inspiration and motivation."

*"A compelling example of the powerful trend of entrepreneurship developing across Turkey – a wave in which Mr Altuntas has taken a clear leadership role and has no intention of slowing down."*

**Hedda Pahlson-Moller, Luxembourg**
*Adjunct Professor of Entrepreneurship, Sacred Heart University*
*Vice Chairman, Luxembourg Microfinance and Development Board*

"Contrary to the claim of skeptics, the American dream is alive and well – it just moved to Turkey! Baybars is a living legend in his country, and will certainly not stop there. His story will inspire everyone – he lives the cliché that "nothing is impossible.

Baybars' personal story of ambition and perseverance – with all the requisite and realistic hiccups along the way – will touch each and every aspiring entrepreneur and bring knowing smiles (and flinches) from experienced counterparts.

What's more, there are important messages and calls to action for women entrepreneurs as well as valuable insight on how his faith has been a cornerstone for professional and personal development.

For anyone who has experienced the bustling business development activities of Istanbul, Baybars' story is a compelling example of the powerful trend of entrepreneurship developing across Turkey – a wave in which Mr Altuntas has taken a clear leadership role and has no intention of slowing down."

*"His success, which derives from perseverance and faith, resonates with how I left Sweden to study and build my riches in the US."*

**David Drake, USA**
*Chairman, LDJ Capital*
*Columnist of Forbes Magazine, Entrepreneur.com and Huffington Post*
*Author of The SPPICE of Crowdfunding*

"Baybars is an entrepreneurial inspiration who is the manifestation of the saying "where there is a will there is a way". Baybars perpetuates the idea that everything is possible. His success, which derives from perseverance and faith, resonates with how I left Sweden to study and build my riches in the US."

To my dear wife, Rakibe,
and to my daughters Alara and Eda,
entrepreneurs of the future

# Contents

# Foreword

**Jonathan Ortmans is an entrepreneur and economist. He serves as President of Global Entrepreneurship Week and as a Senior Fellow at the Ewing Marion Kauffman Foundation.**

Entrepreneurship is much more than a career path or a commercial stint. It is the ultimate manifestation of the possibility of human endeavor.

The entrepreneur's path from startup to scale-up tests that spirit time and again. The entrepreneurial journey starts with an idea to birth the new and create value, and it continues uphill, driven by passion.

Passion for your idea will help you tackle the many obstacles along the winding entrepreneurial path. That passion will help you keep believing in an idea you bootstrap even when most others give up. It will hold you through the many iterations of your product, service or business model, because entrepreneurial success is a marathon, not a sprint.

Baybars Altuntaş took that long, winding path, persisted and succeeded. Baybars had a vision for how to make the world work better within the confines of his business ventures, and persisted through the financial and personal challenges on his way to success. Looking back, many others could have spotted the opportunity Baybars saw in Turkey. Yet Baybars simply cared more, much more, about the idea. He translated the idea into action, learned, and acted time and again. Great ideas by themselves do not lead to breakthrough companies. Baybars' story proves that startups succeed, or fail, in great part because of the entrepreneurs involved and their willingness to go through the iterative process of getting the idea right.

If you read this personal account thoughtfully, you will notice that

Baybars' success is just the surface phenomenon. What the following pages reveal is more profound and therefore important for you as potential entrepreneur.

Being successful at his venture does not entirely explain the satisfaction expressed by the entrepreneur. As you will notice, it is Baybars' empowering ability in the European entrepreneurship ecosystem that allows him to exude a refreshing sense of control over his future. This sense of control arises from an awareness of his very own skills, mindset and vision, all of which were awakened during his entrepreneurial journey. This book seeks to awaken that sense in you.

The joy of the author's success is much more than personal. His role model has had a stimulating effect on the environment for entrepreneurship in Turkey and beyond. Seasoned advice is one of the most valued assets in any entreprenuership ecosystem. Readers of this book should note that, as governments worldwide are adopting startup-friendly policies, the tide is turning for startups to make an even larger difference in their communities.

Seeking to maximize the value of his personal experience for the community, the author wrote this book as an awareness-raising venture. In this candid guide, the author speaks from the perspective of an actual entrepreneur who beat all odds with hard work and amazing amounts of energy and dedication.

In every step, entrepreneurs like Baybars make a conscious choice to forego stability in favor of learning and opportunity exploration. It is important for the entrepreneur to know how to weight these choices along the business cycle.

I challenge the reader to be honest about the risks and uncertainties you face as you read the following pages of advice, and to look for the many instances where this entrepreneur turned a condition into a technique for startup success. Bootstrapping in the early days of an entrepreneur, for example, has proved advantageous for many early stage companies around the world.

More importantly, I challenge the reader to be open to adopting the entrepreneurial frame of mind whether you decide to launch your startup or not at this point. That is the beauty of the entrepreneurial spirit; it is a mindset and worldview, applicable to all economic actors, whether business owners or valuable employees.

At the personal level, entrepreneurship is lifelong journey that permeates every aspect of life if embraced as an expression of one's own capabilities. It is an attitude towards life that allows you to see opportunity where others only see problems. The spirit of entrepreneurship extracts the genius from every individual and translates it into economic and social projects that generate value, jobs, innovations and wealth.

*Jonathan Ortmans,*
*President of the*
*Global Entrepreneurship Week*
*Senior Fellow at the Ewing Marion Kauffman Foundation*
*Washington DC*

# Preface

I have addressed thousands of university students all over the world for a number of years, and here is what I've learned: almost all university students mistakenly believe that in order to be successful as an entrepreneur, a person must have a family member or a friend in an influential position, have a strong network, or be rich.

That is why I decided to write this book.

I had nobody who was in a position to exert influence on my behalf, nor did I have family fortune or a network to rely on.

As the son of a teacher and a retired army officer, in my wildest dreams, I never would have thought I would start a company—without a penny to my name—that would become one of the top one hundred franchising companies in Turkey. Or that the president of the United States of America—the land of entrepreneurs—would invite me to the White House to talk about entrepreneurship, and that the Turkish prime minister, who leads the sixteenth largest economy in the world, would hand me a letter to deliver in person to President Obama. I couldn't have imagined that I would one day be on CNN International commenting on President Obama's Washington Summit or that I would be one of the 110 Dragons from twenty-two countries on the most important entrepreneurship TV show in the world, *Dragons' Den* (*Shark Tank* in the US). However, all these things truly happened to me.

Would you have believed these things were possible if you had seen them in your dreams?

I had no friends or family backing me up, no money, no network at the time.

I could have easily just resigned myself to my situation with a "the heck with this world" attitude.

But I did not.

I believe wholeheartedly that our beautiful world was created to convert everyone's dreams into reality—as long as you dream and continue dreaming.

I am writing this book because I would like everyone, from age seven to seventy-seven, to look at the world from my perspective, to see what I see in it. In this book, I have explained with all sincerity and frankness how I accomplished my goals. I hope that you realize that you are no different from me in many ways.

If I was able to do it, then so can you—and probably a lot better and easier than I did!

This is an account of how I managed to accomplish so much in a short time. On one hand, I am telling my life story; on the other, I am explaining to you what you need to do to become a successful entrepreneur and build your own business. I hope my advice sheds a light on the subject that will help you find success.

I am confident that, once you start reading this book, you won't be able to put it down.

I present this book as my gift to all the entrepreneurs of the world, wishing that it will help release the Baybars Altuntas in you.

*Baybars Altuntas*

# Acknowledgments

I would like to thank Burçin O'Sullivan, Eric Braun, and Peggy Alptekin for their generous contributions to the realization of this English version, and Birol Nadir and Dave Berkus and Nikhil Agarwal and Sean O'Sullivan for their valuable comments on the final manuscript and Ertan Sevim for his contributions to the realization of the wonderful web site of this book.

# PART 1

## A Smart Business Idea
## Leads to the White House

# 1

## An Invitation to a Presidential Summit

I was so excited! Should I wear a T-shirt or something more formal? I decided on a T-shirt. At 2:30 p.m. in Washington, DC, 9:30 p.m. in Turkey, I appeared live on one of CNN International's most popular programs, *Quest Means Business*. Having only recently contemplated the setting up of a Middle East Entrepreneurship Institute, here I was being interviewed on CNN International about President Obama's Summit on Entrepreneurship. Turkey's Washington Embassy was extremely pleased about this event.

That scene was the culminating point of my adventure, which began with a phone call in Adana.

I was one of 150 entrepreneurs invited by President Obama to attend the Presidential Summit on Entrepreneurship in Washington, DC on April 26 and 27, 2010. The hotel where I stayed seemed like a center of international diplomacy. Almost all the guests were ambassadors, consul-generals, or heads of diplomatic missions.

On my way to CNN from my hotel, I was thinking, *Look how far I've come! The US president is organizing an extraordinary event on entrepreneurship, and by being selected to attend, I have been recognized as one of the most influential entrepreneurs in the world.* I had grown up in a household where even talking about money was considered inappropriate, and yet here I was, personally invited to the White House by President Obama to discuss entrepreneurship.

## An Invitation to Washington, DC

It all started with a phone call on a rainy day in Adana.

Adana, one of Turkey's major cities, is located not far from the Mediterranean coast and is known for its agricultural industry. I was visiting a newly opened branch of Deulcom, my vocational training company, when the call came in. It was early January, and there was a rainstorm outside.

I like this kind of weather. It makes it easier for a person to stay indoors and attend to office work. I was sipping my coffee and watching the downpour when the phone rang.

"I am calling from the US Consulate in Adana. Is this Baybars Altuntas?"

"Yes, speaking."

"Mr. Altuntas, let me not take up too much of your time. I'll get right to the point. President Obama is inviting you to the White House. Our Embassy in Ankara has requested that I relay the invitation to you. If you could please give me your e-mail address, I'll forward it. We have a lot to discuss, so please contact me after you receive the e-mail."

I was a little confused at first. Where in Washington, DC was he inviting me? More importantly, why would President Obama invite me, of all people? What could the US authorities want to speak to me about? Within half an hour, I received Obama's invitation letter via e-mail from the *chargé d'affaires* on behalf of US Ambassador James F. Jeffrey. Outside, the rain continued for almost an hour. I felt these moments were the beginning of important things to come.

\* \* \*

"Mr. Altuntas, how are you? Did you get our e-mail?" It was Leyla Ones calling from the consulate.

"Yes, thank you. I've received the e-mail. I'd like to talk about it, so how about meeting for coffee at the Starbucks on Ziyapasa Street tomorrow morning?"

"Great, I'll be there at 9:30. See you then, Mr. Altuntas."

## Among 700 Nominees

As I sipped my coffee, I opened up the topic immediately.

"So what is this about? What is the summit about?"

"Mr. Altuntas, this summit is very important. It is a presidential summit that the White House is organizing. Each of the invitees is handpicked. I believe you were chosen out of seven hundred nominees from Turkey. I'd like to congratulate you. You have been recognized by the White House as one of the most influential entrepreneurs in the world."

President Obama had recently declared the twenty-first century as the century of entrepreneurship in his speech at Cairo University in 2009. He said, "I will host a Summit on Entrepreneurship this year to identify how we can deepen ties between business leaders, foundations and social entrepreneurs in the United States and Muslim communities around the world."[1] The Presidential Summit on Entrepreneurship in Washington, DC was being organized by the president himself; it was to be a highly significant event for entrepreneurship.

I was advised to begin my preparations immediately. "You don't have much time," she said.

"May I ask who nominated me?"

"Mr. Altuntas, all the US embassies received a letter from the White House asking for nominees. The letter said the White House was going to make the final selection. I believe about seven hundred nominations from Turkey were sent to the White House."

\* \* \*

I had not heard the Cairo speech, but I located it online as soon as I got back to the office. I found the title of the speech very interesting: "A New Beginning."

## A Visit from the US Ambassador

On February 9, 2010, the Adana Chamber of Commerce organized a reception in my honor. I was surprised that all the leaders of the city attended. There were no empty seats in the protocol area, so I found a place in the back and started watching this event.

A little later, police and security personnel filed into the room. All of a sudden, the crowd parted, and US Ambassador James Jeffrey and his wife entered. All this was really quite spectacular.

Ambassador Jeffrey had come from Ankara for the reception. In his speech of exactly forty minutes, delivered in fluent Turkish, he praised me and emphasized the importance of entrepreneurship for world peace. When my turn to speak came, I introduced my idea for a Middle East Entrepreneurship Institute, which would serve the interests not only of Turkey but could also help foster peace in the Middle East. I also had an unexpected request of the ambassador.

"If I can sit next to President Obama at the White House, you will see a lot of things change in the Middle East, Mr. Ambassador," I said. A wave of laughter could be heard throughout the meeting hall.

The next day, my comment appeared on the front page of one of the newspapers as the "joke of the day." There were only two people who were not laughing: Ambassador Jeffrey and me.

# 2

# Networking My Way to the Prime Minister's Office

I first met the mayor of Manisa years ago at an entrepreneurship event.

Manisa has an interesting history. In Ottoman times, it was the city where future sultans were educated and trained. It was also in this region that coins were first used, in the sixth century BC, under the Lydian King Croesus.

Mayor Bulent Kar was born and raised in Manisa and has forever remained in love with his hometown. When I first met him, he was no longer mayor; he had returned to his law practice. Any time I visit Manisa, I never fail to meet up for an enjoyable chat with Bulent Kar.

As we sat in our usual restaurant waiting for our favorite local dishes, I asked the former mayor if he happened to know the head of religious affairs. "I have an issue close to my heart that I would like to discuss with him. Would it be possible for you to get me an appointment?"

"Mr. Altuntas, what could you possibly have to discuss with the head of religious affairs?" Mr. Kar asked.

He was right. What could I possibly have to discuss with the head of religious affairs? I had graduated from the notably secular Bosphorus University in Istanbul, and I displayed none of the recognizable outward symbols or behaviors associated with religious inclinations. It would therefore seem a little strange for someone like me to make such a request.

"It's difficult to explain," I replied. "I'd prefer to wait until I meet him to discuss it. Just let me say that you could never imagine the subject."

"Well," said Mr. Kar, "he did visit me in Manisa once during my term as mayor, so I know him. Also, his chief of staff is from Manisa. I'll give him a call and see if I can get you an appointment."

Mr. Kar made the call to the chief of staff to the head of religious affairs, who immediately checked the appointment schedule and reported, "He's very busy this week, but there's an opening on his calendar next Monday morning at 10:00." I readily accepted the appointment and was thoroughly impressed with Mr. Kar's influence in the capital.

"Mr. Kar, it would be great if you joined me. It would give us a chance to catch up."

"Why not? It would be a good change for me."

We made plans to meet at the airport in Ankara, the capital, the following Monday.

## The Man Who Will Save the World

My phone rang and I picked it up. On the line was the editor-in-chief of *Haberturk*, a prominent newspaper.

"Mr. Altuntas, how are you today?" he asked. "We hear you've been invited to the White House by President Obama. We'd like to do an interview with you before you leave. One of our journalists will call you and arrange a time. Good luck on your trip!"

I met with the journalist in Istanbul on Sunday. We discussed the importance of the summit for world entrepreneurs, along with my Middle East Entrepreneurship Institute idea. It was a very detailed interview. We finished with a photo shoot and then parted. It was a very pleasant Sunday for me.

* * *

The next day was March 1, 2010. My flight arrived in Ankara on time, and I met Mr. Kar at the Ankara airport as planned. We picked up the morning newspapers before getting into a taxi to head for the office of the directorate of religious affairs. I opened *Haberturk* and there it was, my interview, a full-page spread, complete with a large photo of me! The headline read: "Here is One of the 150 Men Who Will Save the World."

I could not believe my eyes. The interview had taken place only the day before; yet, here it was. To top it all, March 1 was the anniversary of *Haberturk*'s founding, and to celebrate, they doubled their circulation that day by distributing it free. I couldn't have had better publicity if I had planned it.

We were greeted at the door by the chief of staff when we arrived. "Mr. Kar, it's so good to see you here," he said, and then he informed the head of religious affairs of our arrival. "Sir, the mayor of Manisa and Mr. Baybars Altuntas, 'the man who will save the world,' are here to see you," he announced, gesturing towards the newspaper.

The head of religious affairs received us graciously. On his desk was a copy of the day's *Haberturk*, which was open to the article about me. "Tell me, what is this Obama story about?" he asked.

I had intended to discuss a completely different matter with him, but the bulk of the conversation turned out to be about President Obama's entrepreneurship summit. He also wanted me to meet his son, who he hoped one day would become an entrepreneur. It was a cordial meeting, and after half an hour, he wished me luck, and we were on our way. It seemed that the purpose of my meeting with the head of religious affairs had been simply to receive his blessing before embarking on my adventure.

The chief of staff turned to Mr. Kar and said, "Mr. Kar, since you don't visit Ankara very often anymore, you may not be aware of this, but there are a lot of bureaucrats from Manisa here. Since you're here, I could call around and make appointments for you to visit some of them. I'm sure they would like to speak with you and Mr. Altuntas."

"Well," said Mr. Kar, "we've finished our business, so we do have free time today. If you can arrange appointments, we'll pay our visits so they, too, can meet 'the man who will save the world.'"

## An Unplanned Bureaucracy Tour of Ankara

It was eleven thirty when we left the religious affairs offices. A meeting with the chief of staff to the minister of labor, Mehmet Kasapoglu, was next on our agenda. I could tell from the activity outside his office that he was an important man. When we entered his office, I noticed the newspaper on his desk open to my interview. Sure enough, the conversation turned to my trip to Washington, DC.

Mehmet Kasapoglu is a dynamic young man, a graduate of Marmara University who went on to obtain a master's degree in business administration in the United States. "Mr. Altuntas, let me congratulate you on your success as an entrepreneur," he said. "I was the one who started an entrepreneurship club for students while I was still a student at the university. The current minister of labor was one of my professors, and he was our club's advisor. Entrepreneurship is critical for increasing employment opportunities. Does Prime Minister Erdogan know about your visit to the White House?"

I assured Mr. Kasapoglu that Prime Minister Erdogan must have certainly skipped over that particular news, especially since he was deeply involved in parliamentary negotiations about a new constitution at that time.

"Mr. Altuntas, this is a very important issue," said Mr. Kasapoglu. "Before you leave for the United States, you really must meet with the prime minister."

\* \* \*

We visited the offices of many dignitaries that day, and each one had the newspaper with my interview on his desk. Under normal circumstances, it would have taken me weeks to arrange appointments to meet with all of these people, but with the mayor's help, I was able to accomplish everything in a single day. This strengthened my personal strategy: "Keep away from politics, but stay close to politicians!"

During each visit, I emphasized the potential of the Middle East Entrepreneurship Institute's contribution to Middle East peace. I was also sharing my ideas about the advantages of holding the next entrepreneurship summit in Turkey. I was speaking about the future of the Middle East mainly to avoid being left out of the conversation, but I could never have imagined the chain of events that these meetings would bring about.

Later in the day, Mr. Kar's phone rang. It was the chief of staff from the religious affairs office, asking us to join him for dinner that evening. We reserved a table at the best kebab restaurant in Ankara. A parliamentarian from Manisa also joined us. The topic of discussion was, not surprisingly, my upcoming visit to Washington, DC.

Later in the evening, Mehmet Kasapoglu called.

"Mr. Altuntas, we need to meet immediately."

Within half an hour, he, too, joined us at the restaurant. In the course of the conversation, we discovered that we had grown up in the same neighborhood in Istanbul. He asked me a lot of questions about the Middle East Entrepreneurship Institute, the presidential summit in Washington, DC, and about my life as an entrepreneur. He had already asked me these questions during our visit earlier in the day, but this time, he was taking notes.

## The Prime Minister is Expecting Me!

The next day, back in Istanbul, I understood why Mehmet Kasapoglu had wanted to see me so urgently.

"Mr. Altuntas, are you back in Istanbul?"

"Yes, I am."

"Can you come back to Ankara tomorrow?"

"Well, yes. But what is this about?"

"The Obama event. We have to take you to visit the prime minister."

\* \* \*

At 5:00 p.m. the next day, I found myself, for the first time in my life, at the office of the prime minister. Mr. Kasapoglu met me at the security point as I entered the building and then silently led me through the halls to a door with a sign that read "Advisor to the Prime Minister." There we met the occupant, Mustafa Varank, a well-educated young man who had obtained his master's degree in the United States and who was, as it turned out, also from my childhood neighborhood in Istanbul. As a matter of fact, his older brother and I had graduated from the same high school. *Haberturk*'s anniversary edition was on his desk.

"Mr. Altuntas," he began, "Mr. Kasapoglu has told us about

your visit to Washington, DC, and your ideas about the Middle East Entrepreneurship Institute," said Mr. Varank. "You must share these ideas with the prime minister. We also like your idea of holding the next entrepreneurship summit in Turkey. You should ask him for a letter requesting that the next entrepreneur summit be held here."

I asked myself how all that was going to happen. Certainly these things needed to be addressed directly with the prime minister. The establishment of the Middle East Entrepreneurship Institute and Turkey's hosting the next summit could strengthen the financial infrastructure of the entire region. All this would lead to more employment and prosperity, but more importantly, it could hopefully lead to less tension and less violence in the region as a whole.

"And by the way, before you talk to the prime minister, please prepare a presentation about the Middle East Entrepreneurship Institute for him."

"Certainly, Mr. Varank!"

Mr. Kasapoglu advised me to act fast, because they didn't know exactly when I would meet the prime minister, and that I needed to keep my phone on at all times, to be prepared night and day.

\* \* \*

The first thing I did the next morning was to visit the CEO of the Development Bank of Turkey. We had visited him the week before, when Mr. Kar and I were making our rounds in Ankara. I first thanked him for his hospitality and then suggested we might work together to prepare a presentation for the prime minister about the Middle East Entrepreneurship Institute as soon as possible. He put together a team, and we worked on it non-stop into the night until it was finished. We even sent a copy to the US embassy to communicate the seriousness of the project.

## At the General Assembly Hall

On Wednesday, April 21, 2010, my phone rang.

"This is Mehmet Kasapoglu. You need to be in Ankara this evening, Mr. Altuntas."

The message was clear. I would be meeting the prime minister. I got on the first available flight to Ankara and went straight to Mehmet Kasapoglu's office. Then we left together for the Grand National Assembly, where the parliament was meeting, and we arrived there at about 11:00 p.m. It was a rare occasion, where all the members of parliament were present for delicate negotiations on a proposed new constitution.

There in the general assembly hall, among all the ministers and members of parliament, I felt as if I was on a film set. Mr. Kasapoglu led me up to the offices of the prime minister. There, along with Mustafa Varank, we met Mr. Hasan Dogan, the chief of staff to the prime minister. "Welcome," said Mr. Varank. "I'd like to introduce you to Mr. Dogan."

Almost all the staff in the office of the prime minister is young, energetic, and well-educated, with very good English, and, most noticeably, humble.

Mr. Dogan, Mr. Kasapoglu, and I were waiting in the meeting room when Mr. Varank announced that Prime Minister Erdogan was about to leave the general assembly hall. "Shall we proceed downstairs, Mr. Altuntas?"

\*\*\*

It was 2:15 a.m. when Mustafa Varank took me to the general assembly hall. "The prime minister will meet you now. Don't forget to mention the letter."

When the prime minister exited the hall, he was followed by three hundred parliamentarians, one of whom was from Adana. The prime minister and I came face-to-face when the Adana parliamentarian initiated a conversation. "Sir, I would like to introduce Mr. Altuntas. He has been invited to Washington, DC by President Obama. He is one of only one hundred invitees from around the world."

The prime minister corrected the parliamentarian as he shook my hand, "Is it one hundred, or 150?" Obviously, he was familiar with the story, and even at two in the morning, he wasn't missing any details.

"A hundred and fifty," I answered, entering the conversation. "Mr. Prime Minister, if you could give me a letter asking President Obama to hold the next summit here in Turkey, I will personally deliver it to him. We should not allow the next summit to go to, say, Egypt or Indonesia."

"Let's write it immediately," he said and moved on, wishing me success.

***

It was 3:30 a.m. when the constitution reviews finished. As the prime minister left the assembly hall, he looked at me and waved. I must have blushed a little as all eyes turned in my direction. The prime minister obviously liked this entrepreneurship idea.

## I Have the Prime Minister's Letter to Obama in My Hand

The next evening, Mustafa Varank called. "Mr. Altuntas, please come to the prime minister's residence immediately. We have the prime minister's letter to President Obama."

* * *

The next day, Mr. Kasapoglu and I presented ourselves at the prime minister's residence, where Mustafa Varank greeted us at the entrance. He handed me a sealed envelope containing a letter from Prime Minister Recep Tayyip Erdogan to President Barack Hussein Obama.

"Since you are mentioned in the letter, we are giving you a copy as well. We wish you the best of luck."

# 3

# My Meeting with President Obama

My original reason for visiting the head of religious affairs concerned an issue that was much closer to my heart than this one, but no one was listening. And then, out of the blue, I had found myself face-to-face with Prime Minister Erdogan and was designated as his "entrepreneurship messenger." I believe that God must have had bigger plans for me than my original goals. This is a good example of where divine winds can blow in your direction when you let them. Is it possible that God liked my original reason for visiting the head of religious affairs and was rewarding me?

\* \* \*

On April 24, 2010, I left for Washington, DC, with Rakibe, my wife. Earlier, while waiting to board our flight, my mind and my eyes had been fixed on my briefcase. In it was the letter from the prime minister of Turkey to the president of the United States. If anything were to happen to that letter, it would be a disaster for Turkish entrepreneurship—and a major embarrassment for me.

Prime Minister Erdogan's message was clear: though he could have sent the letter through official channels, he chose to entrust the delivery to me, an entrepreneur. By doing things this way, he was showing his trust in Turkish entrepreneurs and indicating that they could assume a role in diplomacy.

With this subtle message firmly ensconced in my mind, I thought to myself: *If I can't even hold onto the letter, what good would I be as* one of the *"150 men who would save the world"?* I carried the case everywhere I went, never letting it out of my sight.

We landed in Washington, DC, on Saturday night and were driven straight to the hotel. I went to bed and immediately fell asleep.

At breakfast the next morning, my wife asked me a really good question: "So, exactly how are you going to deliver this letter to Obama?"

The logistical aspect of hand-delivering a letter to the president of the United States had not even occurred to me up to that point. Indeed, how *was* I going to deliver the letter to President Obama? Was I supposed to just walk up to the White House and slide it under the front door? Maybe I could ring the doorbell and say, "Here I am!" Like many Mediterranean countries, Turkey is a last-minute culture, and I was living proof of that.

The summit was to begin the next morning at 10:00. President Obama was to make his speech at 6:00 p.m., which meant I had to find a way to get the letter to him before that. But how?

## Chasing Obama for an Appointment

Immediately, I called my contacts in Ankara, but no one answered. I lost about two hours doing that. Finally, Mehmet Kasapoglu returned my call. I laid out the situation and asked him what I should do. "I'll call you right back," he promised, and when he did, he gave me the cell phone number of the Turkish ambassador in Washington, DC, and told me I should handle the rest. Then he hung up.

The Turkish ambassador had recently returned to Washington, DC from Ankara. I had first met him there. He was a real gentleman as well as a diplomat. He had showed a lot of interest in the summit, so I gave him a call.

"Mr. Ambassador, this is Baybars Altuntas. I need your help. Could we talk?"

"Mr. Altuntas! Welcome to Washington, DC. Yes, we can talk. What can I do for you?"

I explained the situation and told him about the time constraints. I needed to meet with President Obama before his speech at the summit the next day. He said his secretary would be calling me a little later.

As promised, the ambassador's secretary called, and I re-explained the situation. By this time, it was already 3:00 p.m., and with no solution to my dilemma on the horizon, I was beginning to feel stressed. I had the impression that he didn't really believe I had a letter for President Obama from Prime Minister Erdogan. When I read the letter to him over the phone, he began to understand the gravity of the situation.

"Who in Ankara can confirm this letter?" he queried. "Mr. Altuntas, you had better deliver the letter to us. It's highly unlikely that you'll get an appointment with President Obama by tomorrow. It takes months to get an appointment with him, and this letter needs to be declared through the embassy."

A rather heated discussion ensued, and I finally lost my temper. "I'm not giving you the letter! I would rather take it back with me and return it to the prime minister. I don't care about this diplomatic 'declaring the letter' business. I prefer that you not waste any more time and ask the White House for an appointment as soon as possible."

I hung up the phone and immediately faxed a copy of the letter. I understood the position that he was in. He was simply trying to follow protocol, but rather hopelessly. I understood the near impossibility of getting an appointment this late in the game, but it was worth a shot—even if it was a long shot in the dark.

As an entrepreneur, I tend to keep my hopes up until the very last moment. If you have hope, anything is possible, but once you lose hope, nothing is possible. This is why persistence and the ability to inspire and motivate others are such important characteristics for an entrepreneur.

Later that evening, I called the ambassador's secretary again. "I hate to bother you again, but I have an observation that I need to share with you. If entrepreneurs from each of the sixty-two countries represented at the summit has brought a letter from their prime ministers, there will be no chance for me to meet with Obama face-to-face. However, if I am the only one, that would be an entirely different story. In the event that turns out to be the case, President Obama would surely want to thank the prime minister for his offer and would likely support Turkey as the host of the next summit."

"Mr. Altuntas, let's wait and see."

I went down to the Starbucks in the lobby of my hotel and started thinking. *Here I am, in this city for the first time, with no friends or connections, and I need to get an appointment with the president of the United States in less than twenty-four hours.* But now, the ball was no longer in my court, and all I could do was wait and see. I finished my coffee and went upstairs to bed.

## I Get an Appointment at the Ronald Reagan Building

When the summit opened the next morning, all 150 delegates from sixty-two different countries were there. The program was full, with one speech after the other. Sitting next to me at the same table was Nobel Peace Prize winner Professor Muhammed Yunus. It was a gathering of the most influential entrepreneurs in the world, and they all seemed happy to be there.

Just before lunch, I received a call from a number I didn't recognize. "Mr. Altuntas, I am calling from the White House."

"Yes, I am listening."

"Please be at the entrance to the conference hall inside the Ronald Reagan Building at 4:00 p.m. Official escorts will pick you up there for your appointment with President Obama."

I took a deep breath and exclaimed to myself, "This is it!"

Within fifteen minutes, I got another call, this time from the Turkish embassy. "Mr. Altuntas, you will be receiving a call from the White House. You have an appointment with President Obama at five o'clock. We just wanted to let you know."

It was exactly 4:00 p.m. when the official escorts arrived. We quickly passed through the White House security and moved on to the conference hall where President Obama was going to make his speech. I waited alone in the conference room for about an hour, letter in hand, until the escorts returned. This time, I followed them ten floors underground to reach the presidential office, a fifteen-minute journey in all, where we met the president's photographer and the White House chief of security, along with other officials. There, we waited for President Obama.

\* \* \*

President Obama entered the room with the energy of a university student who had just graduated. His warm greeting and jokes created a relaxed environment. I don't know why, but as I stood next to him, I felt much taller than I actually am. President Obama took the letter from me and handed it to one of his assistants, and then we talked about the importance of entrepreneurship in fixing the world's economic crisis while fostering an entrepreneurship ecosystem for creating a better job market. After our meeting finished, I followed him into the conference room where he was about to deliver his speech.

## My Live Interview on CNN International

One hundred and fifty entrepreneurs from sixty-two countries and about three hundred media representatives from around the world were waiting in the hall when President Obama arrived. In his speech, President Obama uttered these words that were heard around the world: "Tonight, I am pleased to announce that Prime Minister Erdogan has agreed to host the next Entrepreneurship Summit next year in Turkey. And so I thank the Prime Minister and the people and private sector leaders of Turkey for helping to sustain the momentum that we will unleash this week." [2]Applause filled the room, and now the world media understood why I had arrived late with President Obama, no longer with an envelope in my hand.

Following Obama's announcement, CNN International invited me to join them in their commentary session on the Presidential Entrepreneurship Summit. BBC immediately asked for an appointment. Bloomberg's Washington studios invited me to do a live interview with White House officials. National Public Radio (NPR), a highly respected nationwide multimedia news organization in the United States, asked me to discuss the summit with them on thirty minutes of air time. All in all, hand-delivering the letter accomplished more than simply securing Turkey as the venue for the next summit.

On the evening of April 26, all eyes were looking in the direction of Turkey. Turkey had made a deep impression at the US Presidential Summit on Entrepreneurship. The Turkish ambassador to Washington remarked on the success of the endeavor at a reception dinner, saying;

"Turkey has gained publicity worth at least $10 million from this event." The total cost to our country was zero.

Prime Minister Erdogan, his extraordinary team, and the trust he placed in this entrepreneur, who pushed through every obstacle in order to hand-deliver the letter, led to success for all concerned. In the end, Turkey was the winner!

\* \* \*

On this, my very first visit to Washington, DC, I had visited the White House, President Obama, CNN International, NPR, and the Turkish embassy. And I did it all in just two days. I felt as if the weight of the world had been lifted from my shoulders when I removed my tie that evening and changed into casual clothes.

What I had done for my country as an entrepreneur was clear. I can say without reservation that those were the best two days of my life.

# PART 2

## My Entrepreneurship Journey

# 4

## My Beginnings: The Seeds of Entrepreneurship

*"If you see the glass half full, you can become an entrepreneur.*
*If you see it half empty, you will become an employee."*
**—Baybars Altuntas**

I was born on October 27, 1970, and shortly thereafter, I was sent to live with my grandparents in Edirne, my mother's hometown. Edirne is a very interesting city. It is located in Eastern Thrace, where the borders of Bulgaria, Greece, and Turkey meet, and it is one of the most fought-over pieces of land in the world. It has been the site of at least sixteen major battles throughout history and was, for a time in the fifteenth century, the capital of the Ottoman Empire, until Constantinople was conquered in 1453 and became the new capital. During the Spanish Inquisition, when Jews were expelled from Spain in 1492, the response from the sultan of the Ottoman Empire was to dispatch his navy to bring them to safety within the Ottoman Empire. Many of those refugees settled in Edirne.[3]

Until I was two years old, I lived with my grandparents in Edirne, where we had a lot of Jewish neighbors. I even learned to call my great-grandmother "Momo," using the language I'd picked up from them. When my younger brother was born, I returned to Istanbul to live with my parents. Later in life, in a family devoid of entrepreneurs and businessmen, the source of my business sense might have seemed a mystery, but not to everyone.

I was good with money even then, and instead of spending any money I got as a treat on special holidays, like most kids, I'd save mine. My family would sometimes jokingly call me "the little Jew."

This nickname was not in the least derogatory, but instead, it was a way of praising my ability to do well in financial matters. You see, it was members of Turkey's Jewish community who had reputations as astute businessmen, all the way from the days of the Ottoman Empire. "He spent the first two years of his life in the company of his Jewish neighbors," they would say. "That's where he learned how to manage his money."

My father was born in Giresun, a city in the northern part of Turkey on the Black Sea coast. It is one of the greenest cities in the country, and 75 percent of world's hazelnuts are produced here and exported worldwide.[4] The world's most famous chocolate brands use Giresun hazelnuts in their chocolate. Giresun is also known as the cherry capital of the world. Cherries were first exported from Giresun to Europe in Roman times. I own a hazelnut farm in Giresun, and it is a great pleasure for me to visit the farm every summer.[5]

My father, an officer in the Turkish army, was one of seven children, and my mother, one of six, was a schoolteacher. Both of my father's parents were elementary school teachers. My mother's father was a school inspector, and it was from him that she inherited her profession. No one in my family had ever become a businessperson, so it was expected that my vocation, too, would be in education.

My elementary, middle, and high schools were in close proximity to each other, so basically, until I was seventeen years old, most of my activities took place within a three-kilometer radius of my home. My mother was my teacher all through my first five years of elementary school. At school, I always had to be careful to address her formally, not as "mom." Since she had a reputation as a good teacher, the principal would give her the best classes and the best students. As the teacher's son, I was expected to set the bar for my classmates. I was expected to perform at a higher level than the other students and receive better marks so that I could attend a good high school, but that ended up not being the case. With sixty students in my class, I was, without fail, the one getting scolded. All the other students could go home and had the right to complain about their teacher. But I didn't have that right, because the teacher was my mother! What could I do?

On weekends and during the summer holidays, we would visit our father in Cerkezkoy, the army base where he was stationed. Cerkezkoy was a two-hour drive from Istanbul. We would spend most of our time there playing with Legos or at the park on the swings. Back then, the area surrounding the lodgings of the base was desolate and uninhabited, and in the winter, when the wind blew across the open fields, it made a haunting sound that terrified me. I still get the shivers when I think of that cold wind.

My father lived on the army base, but my mother and us kids lived in Istanbul. When I was ten, my father retired from the army as a colonel and moved back home to live with us. Overnight, the entire dynamic of the household changed. My father would knock on our bedroom door at 6:00 a.m., and if we weren't up by 6:05, we would get a glass of cold water in our faces. By 6:15, we were doing push-ups and other calisthenics. As you can imagine, this was a rather cheerless way for a boy of my age to begin his day, and I was less than enthusiastic about the whole process. This continued, even on Sundays, until I was well into high school. I have yet to meet anyone whose upbringing was characterized by such a strict military-like discipline as mine.

My parents' attitude toward discipline became an obstacle for even the most basic requests. One time, my brother and I really wanted a bicycle, but our parents refused. We were reduced to begging to borrow the neighbor's bike, until my grandmother bought us one with her pension. She doted on us quite a bit and never made us ask twice for anything. For that reason, and to escape the suffocating discipline of my household, I moved back in with her when I was around seventeen. Fortunately for me, she'd moved to Istanbul.

When I bought my first BMW, I registered it in her name, because I wanted her to have owned a BMW in recognition of her sacrifice in buying a bicycle for me when I was a child. I think, subconsciously, I was also trying to thank her for all her love and support when I was growing up.

After my father retired, our routine changed. At school, we would have flute lessons, whether we wanted to or not, and then go to basketball practice afterwards, regardless of whether we were interested in doing any sports. We never had any choice in the matter. Our weekend family outings consisted mostly of educational trips to museums, which were an entire disaster for me. But I soon learned how to turn these kinds of disasters into opportunities.

## Finding the Right Customer for the Hattusas Stone

One weekend, when I was ten years old, it was decided that we would visit the Museum of Anatolian Civilizations in Ankara, which had just recently opened to the public. We polished our shoes, ironed our clothes, and piled into the car for another family trip, notebooks in hand, ready for the day's lesson. These outings were the most excruciatingly boring days of my life.

My mother appreciated students who brought things to class that were related to the subject we were studying. I was constantly bringing encyclopedias to school. After our visit to the Museum of Anatolian Civilizations, I was polishing my shoes to get ready for the next day at school, and I also polished a stone I had found on the street. I put it in a small earring case I had "borrowed" from my mother's jewelry box and wrapped it up like a present. The next day, in social studies class, we were studying the history of the Hittites. "Who will summarize the subject?" my mother, the teacher, asked. Serdar, the most hard-working student in class, stood up and started narrating the history of the Hittites. "Its capital was Hattusas," he said, "and I have brought this stone to show the class. It's a Hattusas stone."

My mother was a little surprised. "Where did you get this stone, Serdar?" she queried.

"Baybars sold it to me," he replied innocently.

Before class, I had sold Serdar the stone for one dollar! My mother made me return his money and then throw the stone away. She then smacked my hands with a ruler and sent me home, which was arguably the harshest punishment possible. Thus was the result of my first entrepreneurial endeavor.

My mother was right, of course. In our household, it was considered disgraceful to even speak about money. When I was a kid, for example, there was a bowl on a little table next to the front door, and our parents would put our allowances in it. We were each expected to take our own share without saying anything.

Certainly, there were ethical issues surrounding this story, but what else had I learned? I had learned how to identify the right customer for my product. I needed someone with both the desire to buy my product and the money to pay for it. I did not ask any of the other sixty students in our class. I went straight to the one I knew could afford it and would be interested because he wanted to bring something special to class. I had identified the right customer for the right product. Many people spend a lot of money on tuition to learn that lesson, but I had learned it on my own in the fourth grade.

Yes, I had done my market research. We were studying the Hittites, and I perceived a need for realia. I determined the optimal price for the product, which is one of the most critical tasks an entrepreneur faces. If I had set the price too high, Serdar might have thought it wasn't worth the money, but if I set the price too low, he might have thought there was something wrong with the product. Hence, the price needed to be both affordable and credible. It is no easy task to find the perfect price for a product, but I overcame that difficulty.

In the end, my mom (whom I had secretly nicknamed "the Surgeon General") intervened in my first entrepreneurial endeavor and performed an operation that invalidated the entire transaction.

## Questions I Was Not Able to Answer Until Now

When I was about twelve, I would get up in the morning nearly every day at 4:00 a.m. and, without my parents' knowledge, go down the street to the mosque to pray. Still to this day, I don't know why. I wasn't surrounded by overly religious influences. No one in our family went to the mosque to pray, but I always felt troubled if I did not wake up and make it to the mosque in time for the morning prayer. I no longer go to the mosque in the mornings, but the reason for my going there as a child still eludes me to this day.

There used to be a magazine called *The Bridge*. When I was thirteen, I wrote an article about the creation of man and sent it to them. It was an odd topic for someone my age to be concerned with, but it was something I used to think about a lot, even in elementary school. My article was published, and I received a letter from the editor with suggestions for further reading and a request to meet me. I never got around to reading the books they recommended or to meeting with them, but I still remember to this day how important that letter made me feel.

Even though I hadn't managed to get a high enough score on the national exams to get into the private high schools, I was a good student. My strongest subject was math, and I received top grades in that subject every semester. Each year, I had a different teacher. In my second year of high school, my teacher assigned me a project that was beyond the normally accepted curriculum for a high school student. The project was "displaying quadratic equations with two unknowns on the coordinate axis." My teacher was so impressed with my finished project that he personally delivered it to the prestigious Turkish Scientific and Technological Research Council of Turkey (TUBITAK). Later that year, the school principal asked me to teach the class when my teacher was unable to come to school for lengthy period of time. No matter how well I did in school, however, unless I was at the top of my class, it wasn't good enough for my parents. When I made the honor roll, they would always tell me I had "done my duty."

During my last year of junior high, I took an exam to enter the highly esteemed Kuleli military high school. I really wanted to be an army officer like my father. I placed seventy-eighth out of five thousand applicants, which put me in the top 2 percent. Then I moved on to the oral interview and sports exams and passed those, too. The last stage was a ten-day series of physical examinations. They gave us a checklist, and we had to visit twenty different doctors. If all twenty stamped your checklist with "satisfactory," you could register at the Kuleli military school. The doctor who examined me on the very last day determined that I didn't make the grade. Just the night before, I had been so excited at having been okayed by all the other nineteen doctors that I could barely sleep, and I actually had a dream about becoming an officer. I was heartbroken by the twentieth doctor's verdict.

Apparently, I had a two-millimeter gap between two of my vertebrae instead of the normal one-millimeter. This congenital orthopedic irregularity would not allow me to carry heavy loads and thus eliminated me from the running. I cried about this rejection for days. The interesting thing is that, at the time, the commander of the military school was a close friend of my father's. I even took the exam with the commander's son. But my dad didn't try to persuade his friend to intervene on my behalf, because he believed that all things happen for a reason. I later registered at a local high school instead.

If things hadn't turned out the way they did, this would be a much different book—maybe *Memoirs of a Colonel*.

## The Carpet Store and the Card Game

One day, I was walking past a carpet shop on my way home from school when I noticed the shopkeeper trying to explain something to a tourist, but he was having trouble because of the language barrier. I stepped in and helped translate for the shopkeeper. After the transaction, he said, "If you come here and help me with sales every evening, I'll give you a 10 percent commission."

That was in May of my senior year in high school, and back then, I would meet up with my girlfriend every day after class. But now I had a job, so I wrote her a note to break up with her. This is how love goes when you are an entrepreneur.

The next evening, a tourist couple from Germany stopped by the carpet shop. After about an hour of shopping and haggling, they ended up buying a carpet for $25,000. My commission on the sale came to $2,500. Words cannot explain how elated I was. In less than an hour, I made what my mother would earn in three months. This was far better than my weekly allowance, which would only have bought me a bottle of cola.

That weekend, I went shopping and came home with a lot of new things: an Adidas tracksuit, expensive new sport shoes, a stylish new shirt and pants, and so on. Still, I had spent less than $500. I kept the rest on me at all times, even when I slept. I worked at the carpet shop every evening and even offered to open the store on Sundays so I could work a whole day.

Later, with the remaining $2,000 burning a hole in my pocket, I visited the local amusement park. There was a game there called three cards, and it was beginning to draw a crowd. I watched closely for a while and started to think I had it figured out. For the last half hour, I had guessed nearly all of the cards correctly. I decided to give it a try. In less than fifteen minutes, I lost every cent. I remember two guys having to carry me home, I was so distressed. I didn't want to get out of bed for the next two weeks. I hated the world.

I had just graduated from a life lesson that cost me $2,000. What I learned was that money can be easily earned and just as easily lost. I also learned that games of chance are actually games of no chance. The odds are never in your favor. I learned a lot that day and didn't buy as much as a lottery ticket after that.

That first $2,500 was the first real financial breakthrough in my life. It was actually the beginning of the road that led me to the White House.

## Selling Postcards at the Blue Mosque

During my senior year, all of the classes I deemed to be useless (physical education, art, civics and national security, and the like) met on Tuesdays. I chose to skip these classes and decided instead to sell postcards around the Blue Mosque in Istanbul, which was a ten-minute bus ride from my home. There was an old man who would sell us the postcards but defer our payment until the end of the day. This was the standard business procedure at the time (and may still be today), mainly because the people who sold postcards had no capital to buy them. It was a sell first, pay later system, and this became the foundation of the "Baybars Altuntas Formula for Making Money."

I learned from selling postcards that I didn't need to have money to make money. So my strategy was simple: be the first one to pay him at the end of the day. The old man loved me for that. Virtually overnight, we became buddies. I was always honest with the old man. If he hadn't trusted me, he wouldn't have advanced me the postcards. It didn't take long for my reputation as a trustworthy kid to get around. That is how I learned that honesty is the best capital you can have in life.

\* \* \*

In Turkey, when you graduate from high school, you submit to the national university entrance exam board a kind of "dream list" of the universities you would like to attend. Based on the results of your entrance exam, the board decides which program in which public university you will be allowed to attend. If you do not have a score sufficient to get into any of the universities on your list, you are not eligible to attend any other public universities. I didn't tell anyone when I submitted my dream list. I filled it out by myself and only wrote down five choices out of the eighteen I was allowed. All of the programs were at the prestigious Bosphorus University, and at the top of my list was their tourism program, mostly because it was a two-year program, which meant I wouldn't have to "waste" four more years studying.

Bosphorus University was founded in 1863 as the first American college outside North America and is currently accepted as one of the top three universities in Turkey. Only the "cream of the crop" of the applicants has any chance of getting in. I figured my chances of being accepted were pretty slim, and since it was the only school I was applying to, I would not be "allowed" to attend another public university. This suited my grand dreams of being a carpet salesman; continuing my education would have only gotten in the way. I was determined to start life as soon as possible. What I had learned from my first $2,500 had completely changed my perspective on life.

* * *

It was July 1987. High school was over and I was on summer vacation. After I sent in my university application, I began looking for a new job, confident I wouldn't be accepted at Bosphorus University anyway. The tourist shopping districts were where the money was. My eyes were on carpet sales, and their commissions were averaging 50 percent. That was a lot better than the 10 percent my previous job offered. I thought if I sold at least one carpet a month, I could make $15,000. However, things didn't turn out that way. It wasn't easy to find jobs selling carpets.

* * *

One day, I saw an ad in the classifieds for a travel agency. They were looking for an office boy. I called them, but the person who answered the phone said, "We don't work with high school students," and abruptly hung up. I called again and asked for the address. I had to have the address. A job as an office boy meant I would have an opportunity to rub elbows with the carpet shop owners. I found my way to the travel agency and met with the boss. He chose me out of eighty other applicants and started me at minimum wage.

I also was helping tourists with travel information, using the smattering of English I had picked up while selling postcards. It wasn't long before my boss called me into his office. "You know some English. I am promoting you to the ticketing department. Go ahead and move over to the ticketing desk," he said. I was not exactly thrilled about the promotion, however. I have always been results-orientated, and even though as an office boy, I was in a lower position, it afforded me the opportunity to mingle with the carpet salesmen. Reluctantly, I accepted the new position. *Refusal* has never been a word in my vocabulary.

My new desk was at the entrance to the agency. Anyone who entered came to me first. In no time at all, I learned that this ticketing business was a good one. In 1987, during the Iran-Iraq War, there was an influx of Arab tourists to Istanbul. Many of our customers were en route to the United States or Sweden to escape the war. I really liked the business. The tips were good. There were three other ticketing desks in the agency, but I was making sales of $10,000 a day all by myself. I was also keeping the books. I was working seven days a week, fourteen hours a day, but all in all, it was a very good living for a boy who had just graduated from high school, and I approached my work with great enthusiasm.

Around the same time, I started a money-changing business. I was changing dollars to Turkish lira and then reselling the currency. I must say, this exchange business helped form the basis of my success today. Back in those days, I developed the ability to "sniff" money before anyone else could. Even when a customer opened the door, we could tell if he had dollars or Turkish lira in his pocket, or if he wanted a ticket to Libya or to Sweden. I was even able to tell the difference between a genuine banknote and a counterfeit one as soon as I touched it. It wasn't until much later in life that I understood how important these skills were, and thanks to such abilities, I am able to quickly distinguish between a genuine and an artificial person.

## An Irate Customer

There was one horrible incident that made me wish I had never been born. As usual, I was alone at work on a Sunday, when the phone rang. It was a Turkish VIP customer calling from Indonesia. He and his five business colleagues were in police custody because they didn't have visas. I was the one who had booked their flights and sold the tickets, but it was a foreign airline that actually issued them. It was the responsibility of the issuing airline to check visas, but they somehow failed to do that. When the confirmation came from the airline, I did not check it, assuming they had done so. The whole thing fell apart on the customer. Needless to say, he was enraged and there was absolutely no way on earth to calm him down.

I pretended the line got disconnected and then immediately got my boss on the phone. He rushed to the agency as quickly as possible. Even though the customer was related to my boss, there was no defusing the situation. The damage was already done. This was the last time I saw or heard from that customer while working at the travel agency.

While waiting to speak to three thousand students at a conference in 2011, I was startled to hear in the opening remarks of the organizer that I was one of two distinguished speakers that day. The other guest speaker was one of the Forbes billionaires, Ahmet Zorlu—the very customer whose Indonesia visa problems I had dealt with twenty-three years earlier. After we gave our speeches, I introduced myself to him. He remembered (how could he forget?), and we both laughed about the whole situation.

A couple of months after the Indonesia incident, I received what I considered bad news. I had been placed in the Foreign Language Education Department at Bosphorus University. This was beyond any of my expectations. I had a good thing going at the travel agency. I was making good money. I didn't know if I should be happy or sad about the news. My boss told me not to worry and that I could continue at the agency part-time. As it turned out, I had barely scored enough points to get into this program. I often wonder how my life would have turned out if I had missed one more question on the exam.

Starting in October of that year, I was working at the travel agency until noon and then taking the bus to the university for my classes. I would return to the agency around 6 :00 p.m. to help with the bookkeeping. Things went on like this until the agency was sold. The new manager said that he could not work with me because I was a student, so that was the end of my most beloved job.

I started working at another travel agency that arranged tours for children. I also gave private lessons on the side. My Saturdays and

Sundays were completely booked. I also started organizing tours for spring break to Bodrum, a lively resort town on the Aegean coast. I set up a stand in front of the basketball court on campus and decorated the entire school with my posters. They read, "Bodrum with Baybars, 90-60-90." Everyone assumed the numbers were the measurements of the models shown in the advertisement, or maybe they thought it was a bus company. Actually, it was my deferred payment plan, where students would pay ninety liras, then sixty, and then another ninety over a three-month period. I was the first student to start conducting business in this way at Bosphorus University. The campaign did very well.

I had learned how to organize these trips from my coworkers at the travel agency. I think I also organized about ten other tours, to the Laguna Beach Resort in Northern Cyprus. Out of all of these trips, what annoyed me the most were the elevators at the Laguna Beach Resort. They didn't work. I asked the clerk at the front desk about the elevators many times, and he always said that they were waiting for the experts to come from Turkey to repair them.

In 2010, I was chosen as the businessman of the year in Northern Cyprus. The award was presented to me by the president of the Turkish Republic of Northern Cyprus. After the ceremony, I was invited to the presidential palace, and on my way there, I decided to stop by Laguna Beach Resort, just for old times' sake. I was shocked to find that even after twenty-two years, the elevators were still out of order, so I asked the desk clerk about them again and was told they were waiting for the experts to arrive from Turkey. That's what I love about Cyprus. There, it feels as if time has come to a complete halt.

***

Years later, after publishing the first edition of this book, I got a message from a Cypriot entrepreneur. He wanted to open a branch of my Deulcom company in Cyprus. To be honest, I returned his phone call mostly because of the fond memories I had of that island and also because I missed hearing the Cypriot accent I had grown so fond of over the years.

The result?

I announced the opening of Deulcom International branch in Cyprus at the first Northern Cyprus Entrepreneurial Summit. The Deulcom International Cyprus branch started out in small quarters in April of 2012. Its classes filled up in less than three months, and it is now considered the most important language course in Northern Cyprus. It operates out of a renovated classic Cypriot house.

## Most Favorite Bits of My Childhood

## How Fast the Years Passed!

Favorite movies: *Black Beauty, Jaws*

Favorite TV programs: *Candy Girl* cartoons, *Heidi, Space 1999, Bewitched, Baretta, The Six Million Dollar Man, Commissioner Colombo, Falcon Crest, Bonanza, Dallas, Little House on the Prairie*

# 5

## A Serendipitous Discovery:
## My Introduction to Franchising

I had the bottom bunk in a ten-bunk dorm room in Men's Dormitory Number Two at Bosphorus University. My brother's high school friend had the top one. In 1991, I had a heavy extracurricular schedule. During the week, I worked at an Istanbul travel agency that specialized in children's tours. On the weekends, I gave private lessons in math, English, and German. Sunday morning was my only free time, because families usually didn't want to schedule their children's lessons with me until the afternoon.

After breakfast on Sundays, I would go to the library across from my dorm and read the weekly magazines. One Sunday, I picked up one called *The Economic Panorama*. As I browsed through the pages, a particular headline caught my attention: "The Franchising Rush in Turkey."

I was in my third year of studying English at the university, but I didn't know the Turkish word for *franchising*. I read the whole two-page article to understand the meaning of that word.

After reading it, I suddenly realized that McDonald's had recently come to Turkey, and one of its franchises had people lined up around the block waiting to be served.

A hamburger restaurant comes to Turkey from the other side of the world, but we can't get our famous Iskender Kebab House in Bursa to open a branch in Istanbul. If you want one of their kebabs, you would have to travel two hours to Bursa to get it. There were a lot of nationally known restaurants in Istanbul that would boast about having no branches.

The article said that the success of brands like McDonald's was measured in terms of the number of franchises they had. McDonald's was proud to have more than five thousand branches around the world, while our local kebab restaurants were proud not to have any at all.

The founders of McDonald's and the owners of Turkish kebab restaurants had at least one thing in common: they were entrepreneurs as well as business managers. But how was one to reconcile their completely different approaches? I began thinking about how to explain these contradictory approaches.

The article also mentioned that franchising was a global system, but the only phone numbers and addresses it listed were in Germany. I made a note of those numbers.

## I Have a Guest from Germany

I would normally have to take two buses from the university to get within walking distance of the travel agency where I worked. I generally arrived at about 6:00 p.m.

The evening after I'd read the article, I sat down in front of my typewriter at the agency and composed a fax to send to one of the numbers from the article in the magazine at the library. I invited the president of the German Franchise Association to come and introduce the franchising system to Turkey.

I have asked myself so many times why I, a university student, was the only one who ever thought to invite a representative of the German Franchise Association to Turkey. That magazine had a circulation of twenty thousand, and yet I was the only one who thought to invite a representative of a franchise association to Turkey.

The answer to my question is very important. This is where the entrepreneur distinguishes himself from the other 19,999 readers of *The Economic Panorama*. There is no scientific answer; all I can say is that I sensed success. I saw the need for the franchising system in Turkey. International brands would come to Turkey, and Turkish brands would become international.

I didn't even think about the fact that I was a poor university student when I sent that fax. Instead of thinking, *What's the franchising system got to do with you?* I thought, *What is it costing me, and what have I got to lose?*

Sure, what could I have lost? All it cost me was five cents for the paper and twenty cents to send the fax. That was it, the whole cost of the endeavor.

Honestly, I didn't even consider whether the German Franchise Association would take my fax seriously or not. The only thing I knew was that I sniffed an opportunity and that I had nothing to lose.

A week later, I received a reply from Germany:

"Dear Mr. Altuntas, Thank you for your invitation. Would you organize a press conference for us? We will pay all the expenses."

*Now I'm in a tight spot,* I thought. They had no idea that I was only a student (we didn't have Google back then). They must have thought I was some important businessman. If they had known who I really was, they would never have demanded such a task. I had no idea how to organize a press conference, nor had I met a single journalist up until that point in my life. I had no idea what a press release was or even where to find a journalist. I immediately sent my reply to the Germans: "Since you are assuming all the costs, it will be my pleasure to organize the press conference."

At the travel agency, we often received brochures from newly opening hotels. Most of them were from the brand new Ciragan Palace Kempinski Hotel, so I gave them a call. I told the person who answered the phone that I wanted to organize a press conference at their hotel. They took my number and said they would relay the information to the relevant parties and get back to me. The five-star Ciragan Palace Kempinski Hotel, formerly an opulent Ottoman palace, is one of the most expensive hotels in Europe.

The next evening, I got a call from the hotel. The representative said, "Mr. Altuntas, we have yet to host a conference in our hotel, but we do know the franchising system in Germany very well. Since it is the president of the German Franchise Association who will be visiting Turkey, we would like to sponsor the press conference. This will give us a chance to introduce our hotel to the business press."

I was really happy to hear that, but I still wanted to know how much it would cost to hold the event without their sponsorship. I was even more delighted they were sponsoring the event when I saw the figure they quoted me.

## VIP Welcome for Hans Lang in a Taxi Cab

It was April 21, 1991, when the Lufthansa flight landed in Istanbul. It was right on time, and so was I. The airport was so far away from my dorm that it took me three hours and a network of buses to get there.

I used those three hours for studying, whenever I could find a place to sit down.

The association president, luggage in hand, walked into the arrivals hall scanning the crowd, looking for me. I was standing there in jeans and a T-shirt, holding up a paper with his name written on it.

He thought I was the transfer person and asked for Mr. Altuntas.

I didn't say a word. I thought it would be better to tell him I was Mr. Altuntas once we got into the taxi, or else he might turn around and get back onto the same plane he had just arrived on. In the taxi, I explained to him that I was Mr. Altuntas, and he got very upset. Seeing how annoyed he was, I thought to myself, *Thank God we didn't take the bus!* Back then, on a university student's budget, taking a taxi was the equivalent of me, today, sending someone a first-class airline ticket. Thus, I don't think he appreciated the value of this welcoming treat.

Anyway, I got him settled into a hotel, and at nine the next morning, we were at the press conference. They were still peeling the plastic off the chairs when we arrived. Breakfast for the press had been arranged, and the room was set up for thirty people. I had the honor of organizing the first press conference at that hotel.

There never was a press release. I got journalists to attend the conference by calling the newspapers and magazines I picked up at the market. Here is how I knew my "nose" had passed its first test: no fewer than seventy-five media representatives were crammed into a conference hall with a capacity for thirty.

I overheard some people ask jokingly, "What's with the crowd? Is the prime minister coming or something?" The president of the German Franchise Association, Mr. Hans Lang, was impressed with the hotel and the media turnout. He was smiling from ear to ear when he saw the meeting start at exactly 10:00 a.m. The concept of franchising was so new to Turkey that most of the media representatives were mispronouncing it as "firenshig" and writing it that way as well. I acted as Mr. Lang's translator. The funniest part of the meeting was when Hans Lang would speak and I would translate, and my journalist friends would try to correct my translation mistakes.

I have enjoyed long-lasting relationships with many of the business journalists who were at that conference. The roots of my high-level media network can be traced all the way back to that first meeting. Since then, most of those journalists have gone on to become top executives in the worlds of media, PR, or publishing.

## I Am Now the Sole Contact for Franchising in Turkey

Throughout the next week, the conference was all over the media, but there were two articles I especially liked. The first was "Franchising According to Baybars Altuntas," which labeled me as the godfather of franchising in Turkey. Another newspaper published almost a full-page article entitled "Brand Transfers from West to East under the Leadership of Baybars Altuntas."

One thing that really surprised me was that nobody asked me what business I was in, why I had invited the president of the German Franchise Association, or even who I was. The fact that no one cared who I was shows the importance of the topic itself.

It was a good business idea, and I witnessed how the right idea could open a lot of doors in a short period of time. In a matter of days, I had become the sole contact for franchising in Turkey. My dear nose did not mislead me. I wish I had had the same sense of smell when I took my university exams.

As a twenty-one-year-old university student, I didn't know anyone in the business world, but now the business world knew me through the press.

# 6

## Bringing the Concept of Franchising to Turkey

The president of the German Franchise Association had returned to Germany very satisfied. As for me, I returned to my classes. Soon, businessmen from all over Turkey began calling me after they read the articles in the media. Every time the phone rang, I was expecting to answer questions from parents about registering their children for one of our weekend tours. But instead, the calls were from other entrepreneurs asking me how to open up a McDonald's. As the number of calls grew, I began to worry that I was going to get fired from the travel agency.

After about two hundred calls, I sent another fax to Hans Lang that read, "You left me alone with all these investors. What am I supposed to do now?"

Here is how he replied:

"We would like you to come to Wiesbaden and make a speech about the potential of Turkey at the European Franchise Fair on May 24."

I lost no time writing him back and even gave him a call.

"Mr. Lang, thank you for your invitation. I would love to come and give a speech. But as I mentioned before, I am only a student here in Turkey, living in a dormitory. Who will provide the accommodation and airfare for the trip?"

"Baybars, don't worry about it. You just bring two of your journalist friends, and all of your travel expenses will be handled by the German Franchise Association."

This was good. Aside from a trip to Cyprus, this would be my first time to travel abroad. I was starting to like this franchising business.

As all these things were happening, I couldn't even imagine that one day my Deulcom brand would be one of the top one hundred franchisers in Turkey.

The formal invitations arrived from Germany so that visas could be issued. I boarded the plane with two journalists from prominent media outlets. We flew to Frankfurt and then made our way to the Holiday Inn in Wiesbaden.

This was my first real trip abroad, and it was to an international conference. I kept thinking to myself the whole time, *Let's see where all this ends up.*

I was staying in the same hotel as some of the most important players in the world of franchising. A British Petroleum executive was staying in the room next to me, and the European director of McDonald's was across the hall. I wore a tie and greeted everyone in the elevator with a smile and a *"Bonjour."* They all thought I was somebody important, but what they didn't know was that I had to be back in Istanbul in three days to take my final exams at the university. I had had business cards printed for myself and was handing them out. I was my own mobile office. On the cards was my grandmother's address and phone number.

The idea was that businessmen should not be able to reach me at the dorm, so I used my grandmother's address instead. It never occurred to me that my grandmother wouldn't be the best person to act as my secretary.

"Some foreign people called you but they weren't speaking Turkish and I couldn't understand what they were saying, so I hung up," she said.

During breakfast, Mr. Lang introduced me to the German franchisers as the contact for franchising in Turkey, and I offered my business card. He immediately perceived their interest in Turkey. I remember him saying to me, "I'm glad you're here." I had been explaining the business potential in Turkey by quoting a former president of Turkey.

"The Soviet Union has been dissolved and there are many new Turkic republics out there, with a total population of 400 million. Turkey is like the elder brother to these republics, all the way from Azerbaijan, Kazakhstan, Turkmenistan, and Uzbekistan, to name a few. You have the opportunity to reach this entire geographical area through Turkey." It was a tantalizing speech. They started asking me to organize seminars, speeches, workshops, and conferences for them in Turkey as well as other countries in the region.

## Founding the Franchising Association on the Run

That night, I learned that if you have a good business idea, people will come to you. If it's a really good one, investors won't leave you alone. I ran out of business cards that night.

One of my journalist friends asked me, "Mr. Altuntas, there is a lot of demand here for Turkey. What are your plans for the future?"

"Next, we need to establish a franchising association in Turkey. The goal will be to become a full member of the European Franchise Federation."

"This is a very important development for Turkey, Mr. Altuntas. So who will the founding members be?"

"I will found it myself. As the saying goes, isn't one Turk worth the whole world?"

"Not legally. You need at least seven Turks to establish an association in Turkey."

"Then here is a list," I said and gave him a list of the founders of the Turkish Franchising Association.

That journalist took the list very seriously and faxed it from Wiesbaden to his newspaper in Istanbul that night. The next day, that newspaper's business section ran a story that covered a quarter of a page and was headed "Turkish Franchising Association Founded under Leadership of Baybars Altuntas."

They also listed the names of the founders in the article. Nine of my friends at the Men's Dormitory Number Two at Bosphorus University were listed as founders of the Turkish Franchising Association.

The news blasted through the Turkish business world. When I returned to Istanbul, my friends at the travel agency handed me a list of forty-five names.

"It seems you are starting an association, and these people called requesting to be one of the founding members ."

Forty-five businessmen had called and left their names in the hope of becoming a founding member of the Turkish Franchising Association.

"Now they are hooked," I said to myself.

## I Become the Secretary General of the Turkish Franchising Association

I organized a meeting for the forty-five businessmen at the Ciragan Palace Kempinski Hotel, but this time, they made me pay. The purpose of the meeting was to provide a briefing on my trip to Germany and about founding the association. That was my first time to be around so many businessmen. I stood at the entrance wearing a tie and holding the guest list, greeting everyone as they arrived.

It all went perfectly, except for one thing. Everyone at the meeting knew at least one other person attending, but I didn't know anybody. Everyone else was engaged in conversations, but I had no one to talk to.

I started the meeting once everyone had taken his or her seats. I initially asked them all to please introduce themselves, mostly so I could learn who each person was. I made short notes next to their names on the guest list.

Seated opposite me was the CEO of 7-Eleven in Turkey, who made a comment referring to his wife, who was a professor of economics at my university. "Professor Ciller understands the concept of franchising in her country. We had examined franchising in considerable detail before its introduction to Turkey from the United States, I am prepared to support the founding of the association in any way possible."

Here is the result of that meeting: It was agreed that forty-five was indeed too many people to found an association and that ten people, including me, were all that was needed. I was the one with preparing the association charter. All the others would founding members.

Our franchising association was founded on September. Mr. Ciller became the first president of our association. president was another well-known businessman. Mr. became the secretary general and a member of the board. The secretariat was located in a small fifteen-so space provided by Mr. Saribay. So now I had the responsibilities of secretary general to the Turkish Franchising Association to add to my already busy schedule of university classes, private tutoring, and my job at the travel agency. I was probably the only franchising association board member in the world who traveled by public transportation and had to catch up on classes after leaving the office.

## The Professor's Unexpected Rise

We had board meetings in my tiny office every two weeks, and at one of those meetings, the president of the Turkish Franchising Association said, "I have good news for you. The prime minister has suggested that Professor Ciller run for a seat in the parliament in the next election, and she's considering it."

"Congratulations, sir! That is great news. Let's hope for the best."

Professor Ciller became a member of parliament three months later. It was then announced that she would become the minister of economy in the new government. Her rise wasn't finished yet. About a year later, the president of Turkey died and the then-prime minister became president. That was when the wife of the president of the Turkish Franchising Association, Professor Tansu Ciller, became the first female prime minister of Turkey.

That founding member of the Turkish Franchising Association, who needed no introduction, was none other than Mr. Ozer Ciller, the husband of Turkey's first female prime minister.

***

One of my most unforgettable memories is a panel at a conference we had been invited to at the Bosphorus University's Albert Long Hall as guests of the university's management club. I had rushed out of class and dashed past the eager listeners to get there on time. I was now speaking in the same hall that I came to frequently to hear other special speakers. I really enjoyed this.

Professor Ciller had been a candidate from the Istanbul electoral district that had the highest female population of all the districts in the country.

One day, after the franchising association board meeting, Mr. Ciller said to me, "Baybars, I am assembling a team for Mrs. Ciller's election campaign. Why don't you join the team? We're meeting at my office this evening. Feel free to join us."

Two of Professor Ciller's students, Mr. Ciller, and I held the first executive board meeting for the election campaign in his office. Mr. Ciller made me responsible for publicity. The next day, we met at an advertising agency, where I learned that Tansu Ciller was a candidate for the True Path Party. Actually, that same day I learned that the prime minister, Suleyman Demirel, was actually the leader of the True Path Party. That shows how much I knew about politics.

Mr. Ciller's company headquarters was very spacious; however, his own office was quite small. He was a results-oriented person who didn't like anything he considered unnecessary. He could fit only one other person into such a small space, and I really liked that idea. Later, when I began my own business, I, too, chose a small office for myself.

Mr. Ciller became my business role model. Even though I was just a student, Mr. Ciller would walk me to the door every time I left his office. I noticed that he was always very modest and polite to everyone. It made no difference to him whether you were an office boy or a general manager, rich or poor. He treated everyone the same and thus found his way into everyone's heart. I also noticed that during the executive board meetings of the association and at the election campaign office, he would never say no to anyone and would instead say "Yes, you're right," approaching everything from a positive angle.

\*\*\*

I remember one time when we decided to take a quick vote on Mr. Ciller's proposed campaign slogan, which nobody else liked, and we decided on a new one. The banners arrived several hours later from the printer, and on them was Mr. Ciller's original slogan. I then understood that, in order not to break anyone's heart, he would say yes to something but then do what he was convinced was right. That was a good lesson for me. If you are confident you have a good idea, you must take the risk and make the final decision yourself, even if others oppose it.

Mr. Ciller would pick me up in downtown Istanbul in his Ford, and we would drive to the campaign headquarters. When we arrived, there would be a crowd welcoming us. There were thousands of people at our first meeting. It was like a movie. Everyone treated him with the utmost respect and deference. Mr. Ciller, with his Ray-Ban sunglasses, looked like a movie star. It was all very entertaining, the fanfare with which we were greeted and then later sent off.

Mr. Ciller was a man who knew how to ingratiate himself in a short period of time and was a very special person for me. To this day, I walk people to the door when they leave my office, and I owe this custom to the influence of Mr. Ciller. In the time I spent on the campaign, I also learned that there is no need to get into politics! As a matter of fact, entrepreneurs should stay out of politics; yet there is no harm in staying close to politicians. If, on the other hand, you do intend to go into politics, making high-level connections is an absolute must. Otherwise, you will spend forty years of your life achieving nothing more than county manager level. Then, one day, a university student will show up and you will have to defer to him.

***

Professor Ciller's appointment as economy minister coincided with the Turkish Franchising Association's general assembly. Mr. Ciller stated that he would no longer be able to be an active member of the association because of his wife's position in the government. As the other board members were less than enthusiastic, a new board was selected. I seized the opportunity and gave up my role as secretary general on the pretext that I needed more time to study for my classes. Most of the members weren't even aware that I was a student. I had been generally accepted as a young CEO.

In a short time, I had been able to meet and befriend high-level business executives, and I became a star of the business press. The editors-in-chief of various newspapers would call me to get them an appointment with Mr. and Mrs. Ciller. They used to believe we were hanging around together all the time. It wasn't anything like that. I saw Mr. Ciller nearly every day, but I had only seen Mrs. Ciller at the university. Other than that, I hadn't had the chance to meet her.

One day, I opened the newspaper and on the economy page, I saw this: "Ozer Ciller's Chief of Staff Becomes Tourism Magnate." This was completely false. I can't even begin to describe the mood in the air at the university. When Mr. Ciller didn't publicly deny the whole thing, everyone in the business press assumed that it was true. I didn't even get a chance to see Mr. Ciller again after Mrs. Ciller became prime minister.

***

The Turkish Franchising Association (UFRAD) is now the only non-governmental organization representing all sectors and was started by a university student. UFRAD is Turkey's representative to the World Franchise Federation. The Turkish Franchising Association, one of the most active members of the European Franchise Federation, generates hundreds of thousands of dollars of income through magazines, broadcasts, and fairs, and its foundation was initiated by a twenty-five-cent fax sent by a naïve but precocious university student.

What pleases me the most is that 80 percent of the association that I founded originally consisted of representatives of global brands, whereas today, representatives of local brands constitute as much as 50 percent. Global brands came to Turkey, and Turkish entrepreneurs quickly understood that franchises were something altogether different from branches.

# 7

## Starting a Company with Only $400

I got off the bus in Istanbul near the Turkish Franchising Association one day and decided to stop by to see how things were going. When I got there, the building superintendent told me the association office had moved to a location more convenient for the current administration.

The next day, I stopped by Azmi Saribay's company headquarters. Mr. Saribay had built his company from the ground up and completely revolutionized the real estate business in Turkey. He was no longer the vice president of the Turkish Franchising Association, but he owned the building where the association's headquarters used to be.

"Mr. Saribay, the association has vacated their office. Do you have any plans for it?"

"I don't know."

"I have a plan."

"Let's hear it."

"Let's turn that room into a sales office. We'll offer staff training for travel agencies there!"

Since I had experience working at travel agencies, I knew that finding qualified staff was a real problem in the tourism sector. A tourism boom in Turkey was expected back in 1990, but the only training programs in the field of tourism were for hotel staff, no others. All of the vocational schools and the tourism management schools were focusing exclusively on hotels. Yet there were about three thousand travel agencies throughout the country that needed trained professionals who could handle reservations, tour sales, and rental car contracts, and who could organize conferences.

"Baybars, it won't work," he countered. "No one in Turkey is going to pay for a course, only to end up working as a clerk in a travel agency."

At the time, Mr. Saribay was offering courses in real estate in the same building where I wanted to hold my travel agent courses. I figured if people were willing to pay for a course in how to be a real estate agent, why wouldn't they pay for a course in how to be a travel agent? I pointed out that both businesses operated on commission, but that didn't persuade him.

My goal when I graduated from the university was to be the manager of the tourism courses I was proposing with a high salary provided by Mr. Saribay. Instead of starting out as a trainee, I wanted to become a manager straightaway, if Mr. Saribay allowed it. My target salary was $1,000 per month.

Things didn't quite work out that way, however. I visited Mr. Saribay many times to make my case, but he never changed his mind. Finally, he got fed up.

"How much money have you got?"

"I have $400, Mr. Saribay, from my private lessons."

"That's good enough," he said. "Now, you go ahead and place an ad in the paper with this $400 of yours. That way, you'll get rid of your $400 and I will be rid of you."

I hadn't expected that kind of response at all. He wanted me to hand over all of my savings! I told him I needed to think about it for a while. It was one thing to plan a project with someone else's money, but entirely another when the money is yours. With your own money, you need time to think. I took that into consideration years later on the *Dragons' Den* TV program, where entrepreneurs were proposing the creation of a business with investors' money. I never failed to assess whether the entrepreneurs had or were willing to risk their own capital.

Here is what went through my mind as I pondered Mr. Saribay's suggestion: *I have $400 and I am taking the bus now. If I lose my $400, I will still be taking the bus. So what difference does it make? It would take me only twenty hours to make that money again by tutoring. If I lose my money, I'll just have to earn it again by tutoring more students and sleeping less.* All I would actually be losing was sleep.

"Mr. Saribay, I've made up my mind. Let's place the ad."

"Okay, then. Go sit down at the computer and prepare your advertisement. Do it before you change your mind. But be careful, don't say it's training for travel agency clerks. People don't want to attend a course only to become clerks. You should call it a tour operator course."

"How about I call it a *professional* tour operator *seminar*?"

"That sounds even better."

My $400 got me a small, two-column space of ten centimeters. I didn't have the money on me, so Mr. Saribay ran the ad and agreed to let me pay him back later. But first, he made me sign a promissory note to reimburse him the following week. By doing things this way, he was essentially sending the message that friendship and business are two different things.

* * *

It was Sunday, February 9, 1992 when the first tour operator seminar ad in Turkey appeared in a newspaper. Mr. Saribay told me I could use the phones in his office and the former Turkish Franchising Association office to run my business, free of charge.

That weekend, I was staying at my grandmother's house. I got up early the day the ad ran, full of enthusiasm, and was at the office by 8:00 a.m.

We would see who was right: me or Mr. Saribay.

In exactly one week, I was counting the cash I had in my newly purchased safe: exactly $17,400! Yes, you read that right. Seventy-two people registered for the seminar that week, and the next week, I was able to add another $35,000. By the end of the month, I had around $100,000 in cash in that safe.

I calculated that about $95,000 of the money I made that month was profit. The expenses added up this way: $800 for two newspaper ads, $840 to hire a teacher for forty-two hours, and $3,000 to rent a conference room in a hotel for three consecutive weekends (since I would not be able to fit that many people in my tiny office).

My initial dream salary of $1,000 a month was long gone. Now I had $95,000.

## I Opened My First Branch in Izmir Three Months Later

Mr. Saribay regularly stopped by my office to see how things were going. My answer was always "not bad." I did not want him to start asking for rent, so I kept beating around the bush, changing the subject to my studies—anything to steer him off topic.

One day, his secretary called and connected me to him.

"How can I help you, Mr. Saribay?"

"Baybars, how is the business going?"

"Well, it's going, Mr. Saribay. In the meantime, my school load got heavier, with finals, and papers, and those sorts of things."

"Forget about the classes; I am asking about the business."

"Uh, not bad ..."

"What do you mean 'not bad'? I heard you bought a car. Is that right?"

The office boys in the building had lost no time in spreading the news.

"I think you'd better come over. We need to talk."

The next day, I left Mr. Saribay's office with a rental contract in my hands and a cash receipt for three months' rent.

\* \* \*

About three months later, I opened a Deulcom branch in Izmir, Turkey's third-largest city, situated on the Aegean coast. Three months after that, I opened the yet another branch in Ankara, the capital. Within nine months, I had three branches, four thousand graduates, and quite a large sum of cash in my pocket.

A year after I'd placed my first newspaper ad, I was being driven to the university campus for class in my brand-new '94 model BMW. Something I will never forget is how my friends at the dorm would joke around and tell me that my chauffeur was downstairs waiting for me. I was eventually asked to leave the dormitory by the secretary general of the university. Seeing that I had a BMW and a chauffer now, and that I was paying next to nothing to stay at the dorm, he advised me to find my own place so that another student could utilize my place in the dorm.

Shortly afterwards, I moved into my own apartment. My dormitory life had ended.

## Come On, Young Man, Let's Go to Court!

One day, I received a visit from an inspector from the ministry of education office.

"Where is your permit for this course?"

"I need a permit?"

It seemed that according to the law, in order to run a course, a permit was required.

"Really, I had no idea. If I had known, I certainly would have gotten one."

They sent the case over to the prosecutor's office, asking for between six months and two years' imprisonment. Here we go; now I had to deal with the courts.

They filed separate charges for each of my course venues: Istanbul, Izmir, and Ankara were all separate cases. I ended up wandering through the courts with a little help from my young lawyer, a recent graduate. Each time I went before the judge, I explained that I was just a poor university student and how hard conditions had been for me growing up. I even explained what I had to go through to get my allowance from my parents. I begged them to forgive me and swore never to make the same mistake again. My lawyer just kept saying, "I totally agree," as if *she* were the one on trial!

Thank goodness our courts move very slowly.

I thought to myself, *Instead of spending so much time in court, wouldn't it be a smarter strategy to spend that time getting the appropriate permits?* So I petitioned all the directors at the ministry of education and initiated the procedures. I finally received the permits and presented them to the judge, and the lawsuits were dropped. Of course, this situation forced me to learn about permits and procedures. If the ministry of education had not filed charges against me, I believe Turkey would have been deprived of the products that an entrepreneur like me would be able to offer. We have a saying in Turkey: "A bad neighbor can push you to become a house owner," which means that unfavorable circumstances may force you to do something you had not originally intended to do, such as buying a new house to escape from undesirable neighbors.

By offering the first official professional tour operator certification program in Turkey, I ushered in a new era at the ministry of education, where, until then, they had dealt only with courses in English, computers, and sewing.

The people at the ministry of education were both surprised and skeptical. Could a private course educate people to work in travel agencies, and if so, then why hadn't anyone thought of it before now? Is a university student up to this task? Were the contents of the course program suitable?

As soon as the program was approved, Deulcom was able to offer certification validated by the ministry.

After this experience, I understood that it's easier to get NASA to send a rocket into space than to get approval for a brand-new program from the ministry of education. But it finally happened!

Although it was painful to have to deal with all these bureaucratic procedures, I did get some peace of mind. When I first founded my business, I was concerned that competition would spring up and force me to struggle against them instead of properly expanding my business. With all the procedures and headaches it takes to get official certification, I was sure no one else would go through all of that unless they absolutely had to, so I was fairly confident competition would not be an issue, thanks to bureaucracy.

Still, to this day, I am convinced that the bureaucratic headache that I was forced to endure was the insurance for my company's success.

Indeed, twenty years have passed and nothing has changed: I still have no competitors.

## Next: Flight Attendant Courses

Private airline companies were just getting off the ground in Turkey, and flight attendants were in high demand. Turkish Airlines was the only institution that had an established training program, and that was only for their own flight attendants.

I perceived a gap in the market that urgently needed to be

addressed. I was now knowledgeable about how to go about getting a new program approved by the ministry of education. Even though the process was irksome to me, I knew that students who hadn't managed to get into a university would be lining up to take this course at Deulcom. Just as I had predicted, three thousand flight attendants graduated from Deulcom's centers in Istanbul, Izmir, and Ankara that first year.

So at the age of twenty-four, I became the first person in Turkey to offer ministry-approved flight attendant courses.

\* \* \*

While I was doing all of this, I was also trying to deal with my university courses. I had been putting off my education for a time, leaving some courses for later semesters. At the same time, I was trying not to have to deal with our country's compulsory military service. I had hundreds of people working for me, but I had no one working next to me. I was on my own. A twelve-month stint in the army would have meant a total disaster for me at that time.

## Remember the General Manager who Fired Me?

In the meantime, the business was going at full speed, and then one day, I received an interesting phone call.

"I don't know if you will remember me, Mr. Altuntas. I was your manager a few years ago."

In 1988, the travel agency where I worked was sold to a tourism company. The manager of the tourism company had called me into to his room and told me the company did not have a system to accommodate working with part-time university students. For that reason, he said, he had to lay me off.

Now, five years later, it was the same voice I was hearing on the phone.

"Of course I remember you! What can I do for you?"

"I've left my job, and I heard about your Deulcom business. Travel agencies desperately need qualified ticketing staff, and I have very good contacts with the International Air Transport Association (IATA) in Geneva. I am ready to help you combine your ticketing courses with the IATA certification system."

That is how my former manager at the travel agency became my general manager at Deulcom. I would proudly introduce him by saying, "He was my manager five years ago, and he still is today."

\* \* \*

Still a student at Bosphorus University, I was constantly appearing in the press; the media really loved me. I had a BMW and a chauffeur, three Deulcom branches, thousands of students, and on and on.

The mothers of the flight attendant students were always coming in to check on their daughters' performance in the course. I never tired of telling them how successful their daughters would be because of the course. Those were the days!

## The Benefits of Getting Married to Your Competitor!

(My wife's name is Rakibe. The meaning of *rakibe* is "female competitor.")

I was against my staff smoking in the office because I was against smoking in general. I gathered all my staff for a meeting. There were about ten people present. My general manager announced that smoking would no longer be allowed in the office.

This created a difficult situation because the only person who smoked in the office was the head of sales, and she brought in all the sales single-handedly. She had previously worked for Mr. Saribay, and I had brought her to Deulcom. She was very persuasive, excellent with customers, and she produced great sales results every month. She promptly retorted she would leave the job immediately if smoking in the office was forbidden.

Over time, every entrepreneur develops his or her own principles. You get to know yourself in the process. I understood that I was not one to be challenged like this.

"You can take your things and leave then," I said.

She thought I was going to back down. But she was wrong. She had backed herself into a corner, so she took her bag and left.

*What am I going to do now*, I wondered.

We were in the middle of our registration period and more than fifty people were coming in to ask about courses every day. There were previous registrations that I had no record of, and my sales manager had just quit for a silly reason.

*I think my body must be secreting a different hormone during hard times*, I thought to myself. *What if this sales manager had had a heart attack and disappeared from the earth today?*

The next morning, I was at the sales office the whole day, selling courses.

That same day, two young women appeared in the afternoon to get information about the flight attendant courses. I explained the courses to them, and then one of them asked, "Do you own a car?"

"Yes, why?"

"We work for an insurance company. Here is some information regarding our auto insurance policies."

While I was trying to sell them the course, they were trying to sell me insurance. As I listened, I began to understand she was a good salesperson.

The next day, I called her.

"Have you decided about the courses?"

"Not yet."

"Would you consider being my sales manager at Deulcom instead?"

On Monday, she started working as the sales manager. She was very intelligent and caught on quickly. I cannot tell you how much of a load she lifted from me. Three months later, we got married.

Now she is the mother of Alara and Eda, and the CEO of Deulcom. She runs it on her own. In fact, her taking charge of the company made it possible for me to write this book, give speeches, and do social projects; I owe it all to her. Marrying Rakibe was the best decision I've ever made! I still sometimes think to myself, *What if there hadn't been an issue about smoking in that meeting?*

## Looking for IATA-Approved Instructors

Deulcom's general manager left for Switzerland to contact IATA. Later, we became one of the first IATA-approved training centers in the world. Our certificates were valid worldwide—except in Turkey!

While Deulcom's general manager dealt with the IATA in Switzerland, I handled the Turkish Ministry of Education. The ministry held a special meeting about this program, and the first ticketing-expert course in Turkey got approved. Deulcom became the training center with the world's highest rate of job placements from IATA centers.

We experienced a slight snag with IATA, however. We were able to fulfill all their conditions except for the requirement that the course be taught by an IATA-certified instructor. We placed newspaper ads for weeks and consulted all the domestic and international airlines, only to conclude there was not a single IATA-certified instructor in the country.

I got a US visa and attended a fifteen-day IATA course in Miami, which technically accepted only ticketing experts who were airline staff. Although Deulcom was not an airline company, IATA had made an exception in our case. I needed seventy points to complete the course, and ninety points would get me IATA instructor approval. I guess they were of the opinion that somehow I would not be able to get ninety points, maybe because I was only twenty-five years old, or maybe they thought I had no ticketing experience. And the exam itself was known to be a really tough one.

What they didn't know was that I had begun working as a ticketing agent only weeks after I had started a job as an office boy during my senior year in high school. I had not taken any courses to learn ticketing; I was self-taught, from books. It was complicated, all right, but not a hard thing to do once you figured it out.

Thirty staff members from twenty airlines attended the course in Miami. They had been doing this job for years and most of them had English as their native language. Interestingly, there has been only one person who scored 100 percent on the final exam. It was me.

I made millions of dollars from IATA courses in Turkey.

At one point, I noticed a deficiency in IATA's program. Although they had a worldwide system, they had no computer simulation. I met a programmer from San Francisco who said he could write the program for what I was describing. So I hopped onto a plane and headed to San Francisco to discuss the project with him. I flew to Geneva from there and had a meeting with the executives of the IATA training department. They admired my initiative and entrepreneurship.

I suggested they could work with my programmer in San Francisco and that Deulcom was ready to pilot the computerized reservation systems (CRS) simulation programs in Turkey.

I was thus the architect of the CRS training system that IATA would then run in all its centers throughout world. As a reward, Deulcom advertisements were printed on all Turkey-issued IATA tickets for a whole year.

## All Doors Will Open for an Optimistic Person

I took the IATA instructor courses in Singapore as well and became the first IATA-certified instructor in Turkey for airport passenger services. I then started training personnel for airports. Ground-services jobs were in high demand, especially airport passenger service staff, so I opened ground-service courses too.

It was almost as if I had joined the ministry of education staff. I was in Ankara nearly every week to secure approval for yet another new course. They enjoyed my company, and I had found a weak point in the bureaucracy: it did not matter what you were trying to do; what really mattered was the kind of a person you were. They were receiving me as a university student with hardly any money in his pocket—well, there actually was, but you couldn't tell, and I didn't let on.

Besides, there was not much I could do other than be endearing, anyway. At the beginning, I had not had any friends at that court and did not know anyone at the ministry, nor had I had a clue about bureaucratic rules. What I had done was to figure out that if I showed respect and was patient, I could succeed in that environment. Although the degree of patience required to do business at the ministry of education was quite high, there was no other way. You needed the patience of a saint to get a result out of that bureaucracy.

The interesting thing was, even though I am normally an impatient person in business, I found I could quickly move into "saint mode" when the situation warranted it. I became very proficient at bureaucracy management. I was able to accomplish in three months what most people couldn't achieve in two years!

## Let's Not Leave the Classrooms Empty

One of my professors was the dean of the Faculty of Education at Bosphorus University. One big hassle for me during my senior year was the practice-teaching issue. Universities had to find schools for students in their final year so they could gain practical experience in their field.

I visited the dean in his office. "Sir, I have founded a training center. We are training professional tour operators for travel agencies. We also offer flight attendant courses for airlines, and we have become IATA's training center in Turkey. If we offer an English course certified by Bosphorus University, our flight attendants, tour operators, ticketing agents, and passenger service agents would get a chance to learn proper English, making it easier for them to find jobs. The university's classrooms are available on the weekends, so how would it be if we could arrange to make use of them, instead of leaving them sitting empty? An advantage for our foreign language education students would be that some of them could do part of their practice teaching right here on campus on the weekends. And in the process, the faculty would be opening its doors to the public."

A week later, the dean called me to his office. "I have spoken with the university president. We really liked your business idea. Bring us a protocol so that we can make an official proposal to the University Executive Council."

Deulcom started offering tourism English courses certified by the faculty of education. During the week, our students were taking their vocational training at Deulcom centers, and on the weekends, they attended English courses at the university. The project had been approved by the ministry of education, and Bosphorus University had been the first to develop an English for Tourism program in Turkey.

This project continued for about ten years. It was the longest-lasting project that a state university ever carried out with a private institution in Turkey. It was a source of inspiration for the inception of the university's Lifelong Education Center. The dormant capacity of the university was put to active use by its opening its doors to many a would-be tourism professionals. I felt I had fulfilled my duty toward my university in this way.

I graduated from Bosphorus University in 1997, after ten years of being a student there. I took my little daughter Alara, just a year old at the time, to my graduation ceremony. One of my favorite memories at school was that, by the time I graduated, some of my instructors at the university weren't sure whether to call me "Baybars" or "Mr. Altuntas"—I was clearly much older than all the other students in my classes, and it was known that I already had a successful career in business. My university years had passed, just like that.

## First Flight Attendant Exports from Turkey

Later on, I secured approval from the ministry of Education for the official regulations and guidelines document I had drawn up for job placement services in vocational courses in Turkey. Deulcom graduates, with an English certificate from one of Turkey's most prestigious English-medium universities and a ministry-approved vocational training qualification from Deulcom, would now receive free job placement support. I had developed a totally new concept for Turkey. This model was welcomed enthusiastically by course participants and businesses alike. Virtually all graduates were able to start new jobs as soon as they graduated. With their IATA certificates, ticketing and passenger service agents were also able to find jobs abroad.

One day, I received a fax from a foreign airline company that read: "We would like to interview Deulcom graduates for flight attendant positions. From now on, we would like to source flight attendants from Turkey instead of Pakistan."

Our graduates started working at international airline companies with an average monthly salary of $3,000. Some later went on to study at universities in the United States with the money they saved up from their jobs. In this way, Turkey began exporting flight attendants. This topic kept the media busy for months. When our graduates had a stopover in Istanbul on their itinerary, the media would greet them at the airport and they would be on the main news bulletin. The idea of exporting trained staff was a very intriguing one indeed.

## Founding the TURSAB Vocational High School

My phone rang. On the line was the president of the Turkish Travel Agents Association (TURSAB).

"Mr. Altuntas, I would like to arrange a meeting with you."

The TURSAB president was inviting me to a meeting. What was it going to be about, I wondered.

"Mr. Altuntas, you have made great strides in tourism training in Turkey. We would like to co-found with you a vocational high school— the TURSAB Vocational High School. What do you think?"

I was aware that starting a vocational school was not a profitable business, so I didn't say much. I only made a suggestion. "We can consider starting the high school, and at the same time, we can deliver our ticketing and tour operator courses in cooperation with TURSAB."

Later on, the president of TURSAB announced at a press conference: "We started out with the aim of founding a high school, but now we are working in cooperation with Deulcom as well! I'm not quite sure I understand how that happened, but let this be beneficial for all of us."

The TURSAB president was a quick-thinking man with a high energy level. He was very well-intentioned but not naïve: it was clear that he would not fall prey to any attempts to try to trick him. He was a perfect business partner for me. My only issue with him was that sometimes I would not understand what he was saying because he spoke so fast. Sometimes after a phone conversation, I would realize I hadn't understood a word. Nevertheless, our project proceeded smoothly for two years. Thousands of candidates earned TURSAB-Deulcom certification.

TURSAB member agencies were giving priority to candidates who held our certificates. The president of TURSAB promoted these training programs on all TV channels. This was a good example of a successful cooperation.

\* \* \*

During the years I was working closely with the TURSAB president, I acquired a good habit. He would sit in the backseat of the car only if he was en route to a protocol meeting or reception; otherwise, he would sit next to his chauffeur. I admired this demonstration of modesty. I still remember him when I sit next to my own chauffeur.

## Deulcom Becomes an International Brand

Over the next few years, I launched a series of new courses, all approved by the ministry of education: the first human resource management course, the first executive assistant course, the first public relations course, the first airline management course, and the first travel agency management course in Turkey.

More successes ensued. A 2004 survey revealed that Deulcom was the company most people would like to work for.[6] In 1997, I was the education sector's most frequent advertiser.[7] In 2005, Deulcom, a company started by a university student, was honored with the Eurowards Fastest Growing Brand of Europe award. Spanish investors opened Deulcom franchises in Turkey, paying top price for the rights to the brand name. Deulcom was cited by the Turkish magazine *Ekonomist* as being among the top franchisers in Turkey.[8]

* * *

Over time, I launched many more branches throughout Turkey and in Northern Cyprus. Furthermore, I created a franchising system that met the legal requirements of international business law. From then on, instead of opening my own branches, I set the goal of having 112 Deulcom franchises, and these would be global, not restricted to Turkey. This idea emerged while I was contemplating whether my young daughters would eventually be able to conduct this business as successfully as their father.

I created a whole new business model for entrepreneurs and for Turkey. The basic logic of the model is this: do not start your business by spending thousands of dollars. Do not follow this path, even if you have the money. Start small instead, get to know yourself, understand whether your business will be successful or not, and if the answer is yes, then expand it. This was the formula I used. My conditions did not allow any other formula. For a small start-up like mine, there was no need for a serious amount of capital. The capital was me and my resourcefulness, my sales ability and my entrepreneurial skills.

I believe there are many more potential Baybars Altuntas stories in the world today. I would like to act in cooperation with budding entrepreneurs out there, and we can offer the world many more Deulcom stories. If you have really good sales ability and you would like to become your own boss, send me your résumé, regardless of your age.

Here is my e-mail: baltuntas@deulcom.com.tr

## The Most Active Job Placement Provider

I had already implanted the notion of vocational training and job placement in Turkey in 1992, before human resource departments became a part of daily business activity in Turkey.

Twenty years ago, I launched with Deulcom the model of free job placement centers, long before the advent of employment bureaus that are operating in Turkey today. More than the income that I gained from the training programs, it was the number of successful job placements that has made me happy. There are so many occasions where I have been greeted by our graduates at airports and on planes.

We published Turkey's first job placement center book for our graduates. In this book, we explained how to be successful in job interviews. Later, we made this available to our students on the company website.

## The Stone Gets Heavier

Eventually, the time for me to do the compulsory military service had arrived. Let me tell you one of my favorite memories of that period.

One day, our squadron commander called me over. He had risen to the rank of major and was eligible to retire whenever he wanted. What he wanted to know from me was whether I thought he could succeed in starting his own business once he retired. I said to him, "Commander, the stone gets heavier depending upon the gravity of its environment, sir." What I meant was that his rise in the ranks as a soldier was guaranteed by the regulations of the government, but once he returned to civilian life, he would not have the support of that structure. He would need to find a way to ensure his own success, which is quite a different skill from working for the government.

## The Father of Franchising in Turkey

*Capital*, one of the largest economy magazines in Turkey, gave extensive coverage of my ventures in one of their issues. I was lauded not only as the father of the Turkish Franchising Association, but I was also praised for starting my own company in line with the requirements of the franchising system. I had become one of the exceptional businessmen in Turkey who knew both the theoretical and the practical aspects of the franchising business.

# 8

## Lessons from a Social Entrepreneurship Venture

I became president of the Beyoglu Heritage Association. Remember my advising entrepreneurs to stay away from politics but to stay close to the politicians? I have to say that while I was attempting to do just that, I messed things up royally in Beyoglu.

Istiklal Avenue is the longest shopping street in Istanbul, about two kilometers long. Located in the prestigious district of Beyoglu, it has around four hundred shops that attract roughly one million customers every day. In the days of the Ottoman Empire, Beyoglu was the center of foreign relations. All foreign embassies were located there but were converted to consulates with the establishment of the Republic in 1923, when Ankara was designated as the new capital. To this day, however, Beyoglu remains the cultural center of Istanbul, as it has been for the last two hundred years. The Beyoglu Heritage Association aims to preserve the district's culture for generations to come.

I met Nevzat Ayaz when he was the minister of education. He had been the governor of Istanbul for many years and was a respected statesman. One day, his assistant called to tell me that he and Mr. Vitali Hakko, one of the wealthiest men in Turkey, wanted to pay me a visit. I was a little bit surprised, but I adopted a wait-and-see attitude. They came to my office, we had our tea (a virtual requirement in Turkey before the start of any discussion of business), and the conversation bounced from one topic to the other until it finally landed on the issue of the Beyoglu Heritage Association. The association, founded by Vitali Hakko, had engaged the most prominent names in Turkey and was rapidly becoming the focus of the city's high society. All the leading names of the business, arts, and entertainment worlds have been, at one time or another, members of the association. Nevzat Ayaz, at Vitali Hakko's insistence, was also the president of the association at one point.

"Mr. Altuntas, the date for the association's general assembly is coming up soon. We are thinking of nominating you as the next president. Suppose you prepare the list of members of your board right now?" They did not even ask my opinion about their proposal. They were imposing the task on me.

It was not a job that would be offered to just anybody. Following in the footsteps of Vitali Hakko and Nevzat Ayaz would be a great honor for me, and at only thirty-four years of age, I would be the youngest association president in Beyoglu history. That in itself was an honor.

One month later, I was giving my first speech as the new president to the members of the Beyoglu Heritage Association.

## Stuck between the Mayor of Beyoglu and the Mayor of Istanbul

It didn't take me long to breathe new life into the association. I declared Beyoglu an open-air museum for Turkish brands and received an award from the government for this project. I went to London and attempted to make a joint announcement with the director of the Oxford, Regent, and Bond Streets Association that Beyoglu's Istiklal Avenue and Oxford Streets were sister streets. We commissioned research with AC Nielson to draw attention to some of the challenges facing Beyoglu, one of which was the number of young children living on the street. I invited the members of the Research Commission of the Turkish Parliament on Children Living on the Street. Our proposal was entered into the official record of the parliament. In the meantime, I was organizing exhibitions and receptions, never failing to involve the press in all these events.

A short time before I became president of the association, there had been local elections, and the former mayor of the Beyoglu Municipality became mayor of the Istanbul Metropolitan Municipality.

The newly elected Beyoglu mayor was a perfect match for this position, with his tourism background and can-do attitude. He was highly motivated to get things moving in Beyoglu. I had a very good relationship with him. We were about the same age and shared similar ideas. We spent a lot of time together, either at his place or mine.

The new mayor of the Metropolitan Municipality of Istanbul had been one of the founders of the Beyoglu Heritage Association.

One day, after an interview with a journalist, the newly elected Beyoglu mayor chatted off the record with a reporter and made some comments about the former Beyoglu mayor (now mayor of Istanbul). Surprisingly, the reporter included that personal conversation in her article, creating a serious rift between the two mayors. The newly elected Beyoglu mayor was very distraught; he had simply been the victim of his own lack of experience with the media.

* * *

A friend, one of the shopkeepers on Istiklal Avenue, called me one morning. The shopkeepers would be walking to protest the street and sidewalk construction on Istiklal Avenue. The rainy season had started and the road had become intolerably muddy, which was having a negative impact on their business.

The construction was being handled by the Istanbul Municipality. Since I knew things were tense between the two mayors, I called the Istanbul mayor on his cell. "The shops are going to close and march in protest against this mess, so what do you say we have a meeting with them? Seeing you in front of them will soften them up."

"Baybars, come over to city hall tomorrow and let's talk."

The next morning, I met with the Istanbul mayor, the secretary general of the Istanbul Metropolitan Municipality, and the governor of Istanbul. Just as I had suspected might happen, the Istanbul mayor did not invite the Beyoglu mayor to the meeting.

To appease the shopkeepers, I decided to write a letter when I got back to my office about the morning's meeting, and I then photocopied it and distributed it to all the shops. My aim was to give the message that the Beyoglu Heritage Association was not sitting idle; it was working for them, and they should be patient. "The mayor has promised this issue will be handled properly," I assured them in my notice. As the new president of the association, I also wanted to secure the support of these merchants, and I was secretly hoping for a bit of admiration from them.

So much for admiration! Never mind getting praise from the shopkeepers or the mayor. I'd done nothing except create a major blunder with both mayors! The next morning, the Beyoglu mayor phoned me, absolutely livid.

"Baybars, congratulations on the letters you have written," he began.

In the afternoon, a phone conversation with the Istanbul mayor went the same way. He, too, was furious. "Where did this letter come from? I've been a politician for thirty years; I have never seen such a disgrace!" The upshot was that I lost the confidence of two important people I had previously got along with so well. Building relationships is not easy, and they can easily be damaged through inexperience, as in this case. I had managed to offend two of the key people I needed to be able to work with as the president of the Beyoglu Heritage Association.

The general assembly day came. One by one, our members started arriving at the meeting hall. It was much more crowded than previous general assemblies. I noticed that the seats in the front rows were almost all taken by the Istanbul mayor's close friends. It was not hard to understand that it was time to pay the bill.

* * *

I had some very interesting experiences as president of the Beyoglu Heritage Association. One day, a prominent celebrity who was a member of the association warned me to be careful. I had no idea what he meant. At a reception a while earlier, I had had an extended conversation with a famous actress. Later, another member told me that, as president of the association, I needed to keep the same distance with everyone around me. From then on, I felt as if I needed to start attending receptions with a stopwatch in my pocket.

# 9

# The Dragons' Den

"The guest eats what is served to him, not what he expects."
**—Baybars Altuntas**

I had been watching *Dragons' Den* on BBC with great interest and enjoyment. The program is known under different names throughout the world: *Shark Tank* in the United States, *Tiger of Money* in Japan, and *Kapital* in Russia. Produced in twenty-two countries by Sony Pictures Television, the program has rating records around the world. It aired for seven years and was the most popular TV show of BBC2 in Britain each of those years. It literally locked all entrepreneurs in front of their TVs. It was followed by entrepreneurs all around the world, not just in Britain, Canada, and the United States, but in twenty other countries as well. On the show, five angel investors, known as Dragons, listen to entrepreneurs' business ideas, and if they agreed on basic terms, they would invest.

The "business angel" concept is a new idea in many countries, and Turkey is one of them. I received an invitation from the partner of Sony Pictures Television in Turkey to be on *Dragons' Den* in Turkey. To be honest, I was quite surprised at the invitation, and the same is generally true of others who were invited. Program producers had done market research to find successful entrepreneurs who were leaders in their own industry and who were prepared to invest.

The most important criterion in defining a person as a Dragon is that their venture success should be attributable to themselves alone and not stem from the wealth of their parents. I was a perfect candidate.

A leader in vocational training in Turkey, I was a self-made millionaire. I was told that if I wanted to have an influence in the world's entrepreneurship ecosystem, I must accept this offer.

We weren't paid; they simply provided a platform in order for us Dragons to listen to entrepreneurs make their pitch for the financing of their business ideas. Two important benefits of the show for the Dragons were media exposure and the opportunity to make potentially good investments, assuming an ability to identify the right entrepreneurs and the right projects.

When I visit other countries and mention that I am one of the five Dragons on *Dragons' Den* in Turkey, they immediately understand what I do. If they ask me about my investments and business strategy, I encourage them to read my book.

On *Dragons' Den*, we would meet the entrepreneurs for the first time in the studio. In the first season, we started filming at 7:30 a.m. and would often go on until 8:00 p.m. We would listen to ten entrepreneurs each day, and it would take us at least ten hours get through all of them. However, since each new entrepreneur came with a brand-new project idea, we examined each new case with a renewed sense of energy. Was it tiring? No, we didn't get tired!

Each entrepreneur found the *Dragons' Den* program a rewarding experience. I, for example, as a Dragon on *Dragons' Den*, found the answer to a question that had been keeping my mind busy since my childhood. There were two important singers. Both were famous throughout the country, always at the top of the charts. Their constant disagreements would always be in the press. I was totally unable to make sense of their disputes and would wonder what it was that made it impossible for them to get along. The answer: it was the competition that forced the rift. When I started on *Dragons' Den*, I understood how competition can affect relationships of people at the top. It happened among entrepreneurs and Dragons as well.

Not everything would go so smoothly during the program. Each entrepreneur would come with great dreams and expectations, but only a few would walk away from the studio with an investment in hand.

*Dragons' Den* became a venue for establishing the concepts of entrepreneurship and angel investments. It was a surprise, even for me, that the program became so popular. Parking lot attendants stopped charging me when the second season started airing; kiosk owners would offer me tea when I passed by, saying, "Our Dragon is here!" and taxi drivers would insist on having their pictures taken with me. Even my friends from kindergarten found me on social media, and I started receiving thousands of friend requests. These were all indicators that the program was a popular one and that it was bound to be even more so.

After the second season, I received an invitation from nearly every university student club in Turkey. My life story became a source of inspiration to university students. A university student not terribly unlike them, with $400 in his pocket, had become one of the world's 110 Dragons and had attracted the attention of all university students in his country. My investing in the ideas of student-entrepreneurs must also have had an effect.

## Have We Really Invested in Entrepreneurs?

There were so many things that I enjoyed about the program that the negative aspects didn't really matter. We need to always see the glass half full. A smart entrepreneur never focuses on the empty part.

In this section, I will answer questions I've frequently been asked on social media about my experience on *Dragons' Den*.

The first question is generally whether we were introduced to the entrepreneurs and their projects for the first time at the studio. The answer is yes. We never even saw them before we met at the studio. In fact, even the documents and any samples they were going to show us during their pitch were covered with a black cloth so as not provide even the slightest clue. To ensure that we were isolated, the entrepreneurs used a separate entrance to the studio. As a result, every time a new entrepreneur entered to make their pitch, I was as excited as they were.

Another question: Once we left the studio, did we really launch new businesses with the entrepreneurs we shook hands with? I can answer this question only on my own behalf: yes, and I would sit down with them and immediately start the procedures.

## My Biggest Failure at the Den

Unfortunately, some of my biggest failures resulted from investments I made on *Dragons' Den*. The investments I made jointly with other Dragons were the biggest failures of my life. I was under the impression that if five Dragons came together, we would be able produce much more than working singly, but in reality, we produced less than if there had been only one. That came as a surprise to me.

These failures, however, taught me that there are multiple ways to approach any business and, unfortunately, when you try to combine different business strategies, you may not achieve the desired result.

We invested in a pizza box, for instance, that would keep pizza warmer and fresher for a longer time than conventional boxes. We all considered this a good business idea, and the entrepreneur was a person that made me want to invest in him. There was a chemical element in this system, and the entrepreneur was a chemist who had the right academic background. All five Dragons invested in the project jointly. But in the first board meeting with other Dragons and the entrepreneur, I insisted on my business strategy of "First earn, then spend." There was a potential order from a big pizza company that wanted one million boxes, but I insisted on finalizing the order first. The other Dragons insisted on setting up the factory first and then processing the order. Without seeing confirmation of the order, however, I refused to move to production. Owing to this conflict of principles, I decided not to pursue the project with the other Dragons and declared myself out. Unfortunately, six or seven months later, we had to close the factory because the order never materialized.

That was not the only such failure at the Dragons' Den. At one time, I invested in a social media site, but we couldn't agree on setting up the board or even how to conduct business. I always insist on what I determine to be the crucial points, and if others see them as critical points, I show them. I don't change my way very clearly, but when two Dragons invest in a venture, each of them believed that the biggest, the most profitable, most successful way is his or her own. Sometimes, we are in conflict. In this case, I couldn't agree with the others, so again, I had to declare myself out.

I didn't lose money in those ventures, but I did lose time. I am not in a point in my life where I can afford to lose time. I spent a lot of time learning how to operate in the business world in my early years. Now my time is more valuable, so even though I didn't lose money, my inability to work with the other Dragons was failure from my point of view.

## Protests of the Audience

I was the only Dragon in the world asking for 60 percent of a company, which was perceived by many people as above and beyond what anyone could call a reasonable level. My strategy for asking for 60 percent was this: in the first year, the entrepreneur says he will make $1 million and in the second year, $2 million. If an entrepreneur says this, that's fine, because it is his business. But as an investor, it is also my business. If, for instance, a product requires a new chemical method and my entrepreneur is a chemist, he will naturally have a better grasp of the product itself. So I told him that if he succeeded in achieving a $1 million turnover with a $200,000 profit in the first year, I would give him 10 percent of my shares free of charge. This was intended as an incentive. If the second year's figures were achieved, I would return another 10 percent free of charge. I eventually would work my way down to 20 percent.

What the audience of *Dragons' Den* couldn't realize was that with my proposal, if the company was not successful, the risk was greater for me and less for the entrepreneur. I was prepared to be responsible for 60 percent of the company and the entrepreneur for only 40 percent.

What generally happens is that 20 percent goes to the angel investor and 80 percent stays with the entrepreneur, but if the company fails, 80 percent of the expenses are on the shoulders of the entrepreneur. With my unique incentive system, the majority of the risk is borne by me, saving the entrepreneur. That is why I ask for 60 percent when I invest. If I only asked for 20 percent, I wouldn't have enough shares to use as an incentive. If I ask for only 20 percent, leaving the majority of the risk with the entrepreneur, that person can get very stressed.

I had to give up that particular incentive strategy for the second season because the audience and entrepreneurs couldn't understand the logic behind my asking for 60 percent. As of the second season, I asked for a maximum of 40 percent.

## Seating Plan on *Dragons' Den*

On the first day of the show, we ran a trial episode. There was an expert from London who had come to share his experience from the BBC *Dragons' Den*. In that trial, I was sitting in the second chair from the right, but I was later moved to the fifth chair from the right, which turned out to be an advantage. First of all, I was able to see and read the faces of the other Dragons and, since the order of interviewing was from right to left, it also gave me more time to asses the entrepreneurs' projects from the answers they gave to the other Dragons' questions. Later, the system changed and the interviewing order was changed, so I lost my original advantage a few episodes later.

People tend to think that the most important Dragon sits in the middle. That was not the case. All Dragons had equal status. The entrepreneurs were trying to extract money from the Dragons, but the Dragons were trying to create international awareness of their business profiles. This created an unspoken competition between the Dragons. It became clear that everyone was interested in the seating plan, including me, but after the second episode, no one really cared. That was because we learned that the physical position was not important. Instead, it was the kinds of questions Dragons asked, their manner of approaching the entrepreneur, and their method of evaluating the business projects that carried more importance than where we sat. We no longer worried about which was the best seat, and everyone carried on in his or her own way.

## Dragons' sense of style

In my daily life, if I wear a jacket, even without a tie, I wear a handkerchief in a color that matches my shirt or jacket. I didn't want to wear something new on the show. I wanted to bring my regular style with me, so I chose colors I normally wear, like a dark-colored handkerchief and a dark-blue jacket. The film crew does not give fashion advice. We were simply told to wear what we would normally wear to work.

*Dragons' Den* is the most realistic reality show in the world. Sometimes the entrepreneurs were so nervous that I, too, started to feel stressed from their anxiety. If I asked a difficult question, it would only make them more anxious, and I was afraid they might just collapse in front of us! I always paid attention to the natural behavior of the entrepreneurs, and I have to confess that the entrepreneurs who came on the show in the first season were not as lucky as the ones who came later. For one thing, the first entrepreneurs on the show had absolutely no idea about the Dragons, what kinds of questions we would ask, or what approach we would take.

But after the first season aired, the new entrepreneurs had an idea of what our strategy was. They were able to anticipate some of the questions about marketing strategies. This was an advantage for them, of course. But even after the first season aired, entrepreneurs would come on the show and make the same mistakes that their predecessors had made in the previous season.

Some of them did not pay attention to the figures in their business plans. When I would do the math, I would find different results than their calculations revealed. I found this extremely annoying, because there are thousands of applications from entrepreneurs applying to get on the show to pitch for an investment. They need to evaluate their business idea very carefully before coming, however. Every minute in front of the Dragons is valuable. They need to essentially memorize the document they bring to the studio so that they don't make simple mistakes. Unfortunately, when I figured out that the entrepreneurs hadn't paid enough attention to the materials they brought to the studio, I would let them know I was angry. There were thousands of well-prepared entrepreneurs who desperately wanted to be on the show, so it was unfair to them for an unprepared entrepreneur to be granted access. I never had the opportunity of pitching my business idea to a panel of angel investors who would share their experiences with me and give me advice. In my time, there was no angel-investing system or *Dragons' Den*. If there had been, I would likely have been one of the first to apply.

Pitching to the Dragons and getting a negative response is not the end of the story. As I said in previous chapters, I, too, went to a prominent businessman and pitched my Deulcom business idea, and he told me that it wouldn't work. But it did. It really upset me when entrepreneurs would act as if the Dragons didn't know what they are talking about. Sometimes they acted as if we hadn't created our own successful business. We know how to pitch. We know that you are selling your idea, and that it is a marketing strategy to leave out mention of weaknesses. We know this, and when we would ask questions, we were seeking the information we felt they were withholding.

Entrepreneurs never got any points from me when they exaggerated their sales ability. The entrepreneur should have sales ability, but if they exaggerated it or tried to gloss over figures, I immediately called them out on it.

## I Am Out!

One project that came up for investment was a computer-based chess game. The idea was good, and the entrepreneur was smart. Unfortunately, most of the figures he presented to us in the studio were wrong. There were numerous simple calculation errors, and I started to feel as if I was his secretary in always having to check and correct his figures. I quickly became fed up with the situation. He wasn't paying attention to what he was doing and I could only guess how things were going to progress, so I had to bow out.

Of course, there were other entrepreneurs too. For example, there were twin brothers who came to the studio. How two business partners—twins, at that—could be so different, I'll never know. Character is of great interest to investors and plays a role in their decision to invest. One of the twins was highly articulate in outlining the business idea, while the other came across as aggressive and far too talkative. He was trying to prevent us from asking questions and wasn't responding to the questions we did manage to ask. He informed us at the beginning that we wouldn't need to ask questions because he would answer them all without even being asked. I therefore challenged him to tell me the answers to the questions I hadn't asked.

He spoke nonstop for about fifteen minutes, after which time I simply declared myself out; he had "answered" none of the questions I'd had in mind. How could I run a board meeting with such an entrepreneur? How would I be able to share my experience with him? If he hadn't opened his mouth and would have just let his brother speak, I might have invested in the project.

## Character and the Entrepreneur

The entrepreneur needs to be transparent in his approach and should make the angel investor feel confident that he is not hiding anything. We need to trust our entrepreneurs, and our entrepreneurs need to trust us. If you sense that an entrepreneur is trying to exaggerate his or her position or is trying too hard to sell an idea, this raises a red flag.

Entrepreneurs are also generally under the impression that when Dragons invest, those investment funds will go directly into their pockets. I agreed to invest in a paper-brick project, and in our first meeting, the entrepreneur asked me when he would receive the investment money, because he had some personal plans he wanted to use it for. He was disappointed to hear the money would not go directly to him but directly to the company instead. I don't think I was the only Dragon who experienced this sort of a problem. So as not to encounter the same situation again, before investing, I made sure I asked the entrepreneurs where the money would go. That question was a gentle message that the investment money didn't belong to them personally, but to the company.

It was also interesting and important for me to learn how the entrepreneurs determined the value their company. Why were they asking, for example, $200,000 for 20 percent of the company? How did they arrive at that figure? Some were able to give detailed answers, whereas others had only a vague notion and could only reply that they felt the amount they had asked for was sufficient to grow the business. Then I would ask what percentage of the money would go to marketing, production, and salaries. While trying to figure out where the money would go, I was also trying to figure out whether the entrepreneur had included a salary for himself. For some entrepreneurs, approximately half the investment money is for salaries. So, if effectively only half the money is going into the growth of the company, the picture changes considerably. It is critical, therefore, to identify how the entrepreneurs are planning to use the money.

## Shaking Hands with Entrepreneurs

I would immediately sign a memorandum of understanding as soon as I agreed to invest in a project on *Dragons' Den*. I didn't want to waste my time or the entrepreneur's. My secretary would invite them to my office the next day. I would have my attorney develop a formal letter of understanding laying out what I understood from this venture and how the money would be spent. We would clarify everything we had discussed in the studio and where we needed to go from there. I think I was the only Dragon who did that the very next day.

In these first meetings, I almost always discovered that the entrepreneurs had misunderstood or misinterpreted much of what we had discussed on the show. Part of that can be attributed to the fact that they were so excited on the show that they couldn't take everything in. They would even sometimes ask me to repeat what I expected from the company. What I expect from new ventures is, of course, a clear exit strategy and a clear idea of how are we going to grow the company, as well as how much time it will take. But first of all, how are we going to test what you promised in your pitch in the studio; that is, how are we going to get through the due-diligence stage?

## Great Surprises!

*Dragons' Den* never lacked for surprises. To give one example, let's revisit the paper-brick project I just mentioned. I uncovered a surprising bit of information in the due-diligence stage. The entrepreneur was a chemist in his mid-fifties, and I had trusted his expertise. We developed a business plan. From recycled paper, we were to produce bricks. The bricks were inexpensive and would provide a cheap alternative to the more expensive clay bricks used around the world. It would have had a major impact on the construction industry, and it would have been a very rewarding project. According to my calculations, it could have made, in a very short time, more than $1 billion. More importantly, that project would have contributed to low-income housing developments around the world so, for me, it wasn't simply an investment. It was a social responsibility.

The entrepreneur hadn't had the brick certified by a university because he couldn't afford to pay for the certification process and the tests that were involved. I assured him that I would take care of the fees. Before I could invest any other money, I needed to have the brick scientifically approved and certified and to be confident it worked and was in-line with industry standards. He told me he would have the certification in fifteen days, but three months later, I was still waiting for the reports. I had to visit the president of the university myself to get the necessary tests done. The report was very positive. Because it was a scientific report, I didn't understand all the figures, so I trusted in my entrepreneur. He informed me that it was a good report and that everything was fine, so we issued a press release stating that we were opening a factory. I realized that setting up the factory was more than the money he had asked for, but if that report was sound, I would gladly invest the additional amount without asking for a higher percentage of shares.

Later, I received a phone call from the CEO of a holding company in Ankara that owned the world's fifth-largest brick factory. He wanted his company to be a shareholder in our company and to produce the bricks in their factory. He invited us to Ankara for a factory tour. I agreed, and he asked for me to bring the reports and a sample brick with me. There, we met with around fifteen scientists, and they asked us to leave the sample brick there so that their scientists could test it.

The next morning, an e-mail from the CEO explained that the brick had dissolved after two hours submerged in water! Our earlier report had not included data on the resistance of the brick to water. I immediately called my entrepreneur to find out why the report didn't include water-resistance test results. His explanation was that the university had forgotten to perform that particular test. I reminded him that he had claimed everything was in order, and I had relied on his expertise as a scientist. He then suggested that a certain chemical treatment would make the brick waterproof. The problem with using chemicals to waterproof the bricks was that they were no longer a cheap alternative to standard clay bricks; in fact, they were even more expensive. I hung up the phone and never saw or heard from him again.

## My Deals at *Dragons' Den*

Here is a list of the deals I made with entrepreneurs in the studio of the Den. If you wonder what happened to those deals and whether I succeeded or not, I will tell you that in my next book, *My Deals at Dragons' Den.*

|   | Project | Share | Deal |
|---|---------|-------|------|
| 1 | Bricks produced from waste paper | 55% | $100,000 USD |
| 2 | Pilates academy | 37.5% | $50,000 USD |
| 3 | Social media | 12% | $20,000 USD |
| 4 | Tomato seeds | 30% | $350,000 USD |
| 5 | Travel agency for university students | 40% | $100,000 USD |
| 6 | Humidity technology for food boxes | 12% | $50,000 USD |
| 7 | Automatic ice-skating rink | 40% | $70,000 USD |
| 8 | Hair-growing shampoo | 30% | $140,000 USD |
| 9 | Travel website | 40% | $100,000 USD |
| 10 | Test book publishing | 50% | $40,000 USD |

# PART 3

## It's Your Turn!

# 10

## Luck, Destiny, or Fate?

"The entrepreneur has three favorite numbers: 7 – 24 – 365."
**—Baybars Altuntas**

asually picking up a journal at random at the library on a Sunday morning had led to the establishment of the Turkish Franchising Association and before that, the creation of Deulcom International. On that Sunday morning, if I had picked up a magazine from the bottom rack instead of the top, would I now be teaching English at a school?

Here is a question, the answer to which is extremely important: Is entrepreneurship innate or learned? It is innate; everyone is born as an entrepreneur. However, since some people lose this ability, it is beneficial to create an entrepreneurial course for them. The intention of these courses is to help people regain their entrepreneurial spirit.

Everyone is born with entrepreneurial potential, if you ask me. Every child that is born into this world is a "baby Baybars." Some become entrepreneurs, while others may lose their entrepreneurship abilities because of their environment or the role models around them. Individual expectations, combined with environmental factors, can either stimulate or kill their entrepreneurship potential.

I had passed the entrance exam for the prestigious Kuleli Military High School with flying colors. Had I not been eliminated for a totally harmless congenital health condition, would I have perhaps become Colonel Baybars Altuntas?

In 1992, I had already founded Deulcom and earned a lot of money. When the time came to write my first check, I remember having trouble filling it out. I had to ask the bank manager for help. I wish I had had a course so that I didn't have to appear so inexperienced in front of the manager.

## Entrepreneurship Training Prevents You from Suffering

In remote areas of Anatolia, there are barbers who, in the absence of trained dentists, take it upon themselves to serve their customers in more ways than one. They can pull a tooth from its root in a couple of seconds; your wound bleeds and hurts a lot, and in about a month, you can start eating again. When you go to a professional dentist to have a tooth extracted, he injects a painkiller into your gums so that, without pain or bleeding, you can start eating within a half hour. At the end of a month, the results are the same, but the first method involved unnecessary pain. Entrepreneurship training can prevent pain and suffering.

In my day, there was no such thing as entrepreneurship training. I didn't learn how to prepare a business plan until Deulcom was ten years old. Although things probably wouldn't be much different for me today if I had attended an entrepreneurship course, I would not have wasted valuable time and money learning what to do and what not to do.

Let me make one thing perfectly clear: entrepreneurship courses will not turn you into an entrepreneur. They can, however, make the learning process smoother and help prevent you from making unnecessary mistakes.

Keep in mind that I believe that being able to sniff out the right business is something that you are born with, not learned; but you can certainly develop this ability.

It is for this reason that I cannot see an individual who was born into a family wealth of millions of dollars as a true entrepreneur.

Think of a person who lives in a house so dirty that it more resembles a pigsty. When you ask him about the foul smell, he responds with, "What smell?" Since he has spent his entire life around that smell, he is no longer sensitive to it. It's the same for people born with a silver spoon in their mouth. They can't smell money because they have always been around it.

I therefore do not even bother asking friends who were born rich for their opinion on whether a new business might succeed or not, because they do not understand. If an ordinary citizen says "great," and if my friends who, like me, started from scratch approve the project, then I have finished a lot of my market research already. Of course, there are always exceptions.

After market research, I would prepare my business plan and would definitely attach to it a prospective estimated budget. However, I have observed that many new entrepreneurs have been doing their market research with calculators in their hands and spreadsheets on their laptops. Shouldn't you first try to understand if the business idea would sell in real world? Did I have a business plan when I was building Deulcom? Did I have any marketing budget? What did I have to begin with?

## Consulting the Rich: A Waste of Time?

It is not always useful to consult those who were born rich. If possible, reach the generation where the money was first generated, possibly the parents or grandparents of the family.

Money transfer is like a heart transplant. Your customers generate your capital. Everyone can be a doctor, but not all doctors can operate on the heart. Reach out to those who managed the first money transfers from their customer's pocket into the company's coffers. Be all ears when you listen to them, with the same attention you are reading this book with now.

In the European Union, the underlying principle is to favor the small businesses and small entrepreneurs.

This part is very important, because it is a very big step for those who are starting from scratch. The importance of entrepreneurs is gradually sinking in more and more.

This address is an important one for entrepreneurs: www.world-entrepreneurship-forum.com Make sure you visit this website.

## Those Who Know Have a Responsibility to Teach Others

As a person who both knows and teaches, I have founded the Baybars Altuntas Entrepreneurship Academy in order to transfer the knowledge that I have gained from experience to future Baybars Altuntases. At Baybars Altuntas Entrepreneurship Academy, I aim to cooperate with entrepreneurs in line with the principle of "those who know have a responsibility to teach others."

Follow the academy's activities at www.baybarsaltuntas. com/eng/

Just to re-cap: Those who were born into money generally do not make good entrepreneurs, because their noses don't sniff money as well as those who were not born rich. They can be good investors or professional senior executives, but they may find it a real challenge to become a business owner. I am not sure if this indicates that those people are lucky or unlucky. I do believe the following "Kasas" verses from the Koran that tell us divine justice favors those have no money in their pocket.

> *28-5: And we so want it that we contribute to those who are under oppression, so we make leaders out of them, turn them into inheritors.*
>
> *28-6: And offer them potentials and power on earth.*

That is to say, divine justice is on your side if you have no money: this is very clear.

In essence, what may seem to be a handicap—a lack of money—is actually an advantage in that, with divine justice on your side, you start out one step ahead.

## The Holy Koran Is Also the Guide of the Entrepreneur

I want to draw your attention to the following Koran "Zuhruf" verses, which I see as relevant for entrepreneurs.

> *43-32: We provided their subsistence share on earth among each other. And we graded some superior among others so some will employ the other.*

I believe this is a source of motivation for entrepreneurs. It does not say, however, that everyone is born an entrepreneur, in the way that I believe to be the case.

Below, I would like to share some extracts from the Koran's "Kehf" verses that have occupied my entrepreneurial mind.

*18-32: Give them these two men as examples: We have given one of them two vineyards surrounded by date trees with a field in between the two yards.*

*18-33: Both these vineyards produced their fruits without any deficiency. We had also spout a river in between the two yards.*

*18-34: Then he had a big fortune. When talking to his friend he said, "My possessions are more than yours. I am also superior in terms of manpower."*

*18-35: Then he persecuted himself and entered into his vineyard. He said: "I do not believe this will ever end until the end of days."*

*18-36: I do not believe there will ever be a doomsday, either. Even if I am returned back to my God, I swear I will find a better result."*

*18- 37: His friend replied back, saying, "Are you denying God, who has created you from dirt, from a tiny progeny of water and composed so that you are perfect?"*

*18- 38: "But that Allah is my God. I cannot put anyone before Him."*

*18-39, 40: "When you entered into your vineyard, you should have said Maşallah (Praise God) God is the only one with Power! If you see my possessions and kids less than yours, maybe God will give me better than your vineyard. Maybe He will bring down a disaster from the sky and the vineyard would suddenly stay all dry and stony."*

*18-41: "Or its water would dry out, (let alone finding water once again) you will not be in a shape to even look for it."*

*18-42: As a result all his fortune was destroyed. Collapsed at his vineyard, while complaining about his consumption, chafing his hands, he was saying, "I wish I had not put anyone before Him ..."*

*18-43: He had to no one to help him other than God. He was not in a power to save himself.*

*18-44: It is in this situation that to guard (to protect and guard) only belongs to God, who is the Righteous one. And his reward is better, its result is also better.*

We have to take the following lesson from these important sayings: you cannot know what you are; you should only consider what you will be. You don't know what you've got until you lose it. These are facts of life. For this reason, you will either understand and digest the moral of this event and be one of those who will win before losing, or you will choose to boast about what you have and fall into the well you have dug. The choice is yours.

\*\*\*

Because I am Muslim, I have used the Koran as a resource and have therefore provided my examples from there. I propose that each of us should look to the books and teachings of our own religions for wisdom about money, wealth, and the concepts of happiness and success—all issues relevant to entrepreneurs worldwide. It is my expectation that these will be addressed in one way or another by all the world's religions.

## You Will Never Arrive at Your Destination Unless You Take the First Steps

You will never achieve your goal unless you start down the right road that leads to it. You can make as many business plans as you like, get your projects approved through the necessary channels, and calculate your income for the next five years. But all this is in vain. How can you be sure of how much you will make in five years when you're not even sure if you will be alive tomorrow?

Of course, you still have to do all these things, just to be safe. And make sure you talk to God about all these issues.

I've already described to you what it was like to try to create an opportunity to increase my monthly income from a standard $500 salary to a higher salary of $1,000 dollars by investing the $400 dollars I had in my pocket. Instead of the $1,000 dollar salary I was shooting for, I ended up making $95,000 dollars that month! The real issue is therefore not simply preparing spreadsheets. **The real issue is knowing how to pick up the scent of a good prospect and assessing exactly what it is you have to lose.**

Compare employees who work for a salary and fall apart if they are paid two days late. They get paid without any risks, just by working certain hours and days of the week. There is no risk involved. Compare that situation with that of the entrepreneur.

The entrepreneur generates a business idea, turns it into a business, and creates many job opportunities. They provide solutions to their fellow countrymen and other people around the world, increasing the quality of their own lives as well as that of society in general. They shouldered all the risks and included their family in these risks. And they then have to think, *"After all the expenses are taken out, the wages, rent, electricity, water and so on, if there is anything left, then I am content with it. If there is none left, then we can turn the risk over once again next month."*

Now put your hand on your heart and tell me: are these two people the same? On one side is the person who is taken care of by someone else, without taking any risks, and on the other side, there is the person who takes care of others and assumes all the risks.

I think a medal of honor should be given to all entrepreneurs who handle their business properly, without becoming a burden to others. I believe these people are the ones who should have their hands kissed out of respect; not only on earth, but I also believe they will have a special reward in the afterlife.

* * *

After a speech I gave at a university, a female student who was wearing the Islamic headscarf asked me this question: "Mr. Altuntas, you are talking about how important entrepreneurship is for developing a society, how it is good to set up a business and create jobs. I want to start up my business, but when I go home, my parents are saying that first I have to graduate, then get married, then look after my children, and only after they are grown can I set up a business. So, under those conditions, how can I possibly implement what you tell us here?"

That was a really good question. And it is one asked by many female would-be entrepreneurs in predominantly Muslim countries. *The Global Entrepreneurship Monitor* confirms that the percentage of women entrepreneurs in Muslim countries is significantly lower than in Europe or the United States.[9]

This may be a little surprising, actually, because the Prophet Mohammed essentially supported entrepreneurship by saying that 90 percent of the income is from business. This shows his position that doing business is better than working as an employee. The Prophet Mohammed also supported women entrepreneurs. When he married, his wife was an entrepreneur conducting business in Mecca. He didn't ask his wife to close her business and look after children. He supported her entrepreneurial activities.

Since what the prophets do serves as a model, the Prophet Mohammed's supporting women in business carries great weight.

\*\*\*

It is possible that the entrepreneur will get strained while running his or her business. Not everything always goes as planned. It is not imperative that things go perfectly all the time. Sometimes things get complicated.

There may be mistakes in the business plans. You may make mistakes owing to your inexperience. People working for you may make mistakes. The general economy may take a dive, or the product that sold so well yesterday may simply cease to have a market today.

Since I know the hardships an entrepreneur faces and how exceptional entrepreneurs are, I would especially like to share with you what the divine wind whispers into our ears from the Koran's "Insirah" verses:

> *94-5: Therefore, next to each hardship there surely is an ease.*
>
> *94-6: Next to each hardship there surely is an ease.*

The entrepreneur must be patient when faced with hardships.

## Accomplish Your Task Impeccably; Then Wait for Your Fate

I have met and gotten to know so many entrepreneurs during my life. Some of have talked to me about the way they do business.

"It has nothing to do with luck. I will definitely make a good plan and will definitely win." A lot of these entrepreneurs with that mentality have gone bankrupt.

Therefore, I say: "Entrepreneurs should do impeccably everything that falls in their lap, and then they should know to say 'now, let's let fate decide the level of success.'"

After that, he shouldn't bother being happy or unhappy about the results. Regardless of the end result, he should start thinking about the next step. There is a good reason for everything, and every bad thing also has a good reason behind it! For this reason, I think that immediately rejoicing or crying about events is not rational behavior.

I really appreciate the following saying from the Prophet Mohammed:

"The believer's situation is interesting. When there is a good thing happening, it is good for them. When there is something (seemingly) bad happening, it is still good for them."

I would like to end this chapter with a final message for entrepreneurs from the Koran:

> *94-7: Therefore, as soon as you are done with one task, start with a new one and get tired!*

the venture capital system. Although the venture capital system and the angel-investment systems are similar, there are a few basic differences.

When we consider these basic factors, you will understand that what we really need in the world today are angel investors.

Investments between $500,000 and $3 million fall into a gray area called "equity gap." This band is called a mini VC, and it is an area where neither venture capitalists nor angel investors are generally interested. My personal advice is to consider this gap when drawing up your business plans.

Some market researchers suggest that one out of every twelve people in the United States, one out of thirty-five people in the EU, one out of forty-seven in the UK, and one out of sixty-seven in Finland aspire to start their own businesses. According to an opinion poll that Obama commissioned before his election, 70 percent of Americans see large corporations as responsible for the world economic crisis, and they believe this dilemma can be solved with the help of small business owners. This sheds light on why President Obama declared the twentieth century as the era of entrepreneurship.

## How Not to Get Stuck in "Wannapreneurship"

The apparent contradiction stems from the confusion of two concepts: "wannapreneurship" and entrepreneurship. Wannapreneurship precedes, but does not necessarily result in, entrepreneurship.

Entrepreneurs can be grouped as follows:

1. **Those who need seed funding.** They have only a business idea but no market research other than the opinions of those close to them.
2. **Those who already have an existing business.** They have already built their business, but it needs to be institutionalized.
3. **Those who are at start-up position.** The sample, the business plan, and market research are ready; the business is ready or almost ready to go.

Angel investors are interested in all three groups. Entrepreneurs who need seed funding can find smaller contracts ranging between $10,000 and $50,000; those in the start-up position have a chance to find contracts ranging from $50,000 to $100,000 and attract more angel investors. Those who already have a business are able to attract angel investments of up to $500,000 to expand it.

Even though your business idea may be able to generate income, you still need to pay attention to the following ten points when you look for a business partner.

1. **Angel investors invest in the entrepreneur.**
   Angel investors focus more on identifying the right entrepreneur rather than the right project. It is essential that they get along well on a personal level. The angel also wants to assess how far and how well the entrepreneur will go on his own. In general, an A-type entrepreneur with a B-type project has a better chance of getting angel investment than a B-type entrepreneur with an A-type project.

2. **Angel investors pay close attention to entrepreneurs' presentations.**
   When explaining their business idea to an angel investor, entrepreneurs should be able to present the key aspects of their project in five minutes: financing, the payback period, and the exit strategy. This is called "elevator pitching." The most common mistake is to make a long and boring presentation. This leaves investors wondering whether the personal relationship is going to be dull, even though the project itself may be suitable. And what will we do at a board meeting with this person who can't communicate the main concept of his project in five minutes?

3. **Angel investors want to know the exit strategy.**
   Once you describe your exit plan, you start getting bonus points from your angel investor. In general, entrepreneurs fail to consider an exit strategy. Angel investors normally expect to exit after three to seven years. They can exit by selling their

shares to a new entrepreneur or potential investor, by opening to the public, by selling to a venture capitalist, by selling shares back to the entrepreneur, or by franchising. Angel investors know that entrepreneurs tend to lose their motivation within seven years, regardless of how much money they make. It helps the business grow faster to have a highly motivated entrepreneur in the game while things are still going well.

4. **Know your angel investor well.**
   Know what kind of investments your angel investors have experience in, how well they are known in the sector where you aim to do business, the scope of their network, the satisfaction level of entrepreneurs they worked with before you, how much time they will be able to give you, and their success record in previous investments. Also examine their CV, if one is available.

5. **Due diligence is very important for your angel investor.**
   Let's say an angel investor likes you and thinks you are the right entrepreneur for them to invest in. Now is the time for them to test the veracity of what you have said in your pitch—the due-diligence period. Very few angel investors decide to move on to the contract phase without due diligence. Most decide after a three-month due-diligence period. To avoid losing time, it is important that the realities of your business plan are a true reflection of what you claimed in your presentation.

6. **Prepare four different presentations for the angel investor.**
   The entrepreneur needs to have four different presentations. You have to have a different technique for a face-to-face presentation and another one for written presentations. First, you need to prepare a thorough business plan of 20-50 pages. Then convert this to a twenty-slide PowerPoint presentation for potential angel investors, sum that up in an executive summary that sums up the main concept and the proposed investment in about four pages, and finally, you will have to distill it further to your five-minute elevator pitch.

7. **The process of getting angel investments**
   Out of every hundred entrepreneurs, only one attracts an investment in his project. The percentage can be even lower than 1 percent in countries where there are few angel investors. Below, you can see how this percentage is achieved.[13]

   - The Preview Process of the Business Idea - 25% of the applications pass on to the next step.
   - The Detailed Examination Process - 30% moves on to the next step.
   - Face-to-Face Presentation Process - A face-to-face presentation and question-answer session is often requested by the entrepreneur.
   - Due Diligence - 30% of those who make it to this stage are invited to an investment meeting.
   - Realizing the Investment - Half of those who are invited to the investment meeting succeed in getting an investment.

8. **Know which sectors the angel investors like to invest in**
   Investigate what sectors the angel investors are interested in if you want to increase your chances of securing investments.

9. **Eight guaranteed ways to lose an angel investor**
   The following techniques will enhance the possibility of losing your angel investors, even if you have the perfect business idea. Do not:

   - Fail to take adequate time and care in the preparation of your business plan and presentation.
   - Neglect the business model or list only the specifications of your product in your presentation.
   - Utter comments such as, "This is a quite complicated system to understand."

- Indicate that all you want is money and that they should leave the rest to you.
- Turn off your cell phone during the due-diligence period.
- Refuse to listen carefully to the questions your angel investors ask. Let them listen to you.
- Keep the key issues about the business model to yourself.
- Say that you hope to be in business together "until death do you part."

## What Do I Invest In?

I receive at least fifty business ideas in my mailbox every day. You can also send one, of course. However, it is helpful to know the Baybars Altuntas investment rules.

I invest in start-ups that reflect three main principles:

1. It has to fit the "first sell, then spend" business model.
2. The entrepreneur has to be someone that I can work well with on a personal level.
3. The project should be one that needs me and my expertise, as well as my money. If what you need is simply financing, you need to look for a non-angel investor.

You can forward your entrepreneurial projects to me online by clicking on "Get Investment" on my website:
www.baybarsaltuntas.com/eng/

# 12

## A Road Map to Success

In this chapter, I will give you the key details of each step of the entrepreneurship journey. I have noted what I did in each step by giving examples from my life story, and I want you to write down what you have done in each step so that you can determine the level of your entrepreneurship. As a matter of fact, I want you to write your own entrepreneurship story. I did it; you can do it too!

I have grouped all the steps, from beginning to end, that an entrepreneur will take during his entrepreneurship journey. I refer to those steps as "the rising map of successful entrepreneurship," and I have given hundreds of speeches all over the world on this topic. This map, which I produced for world-class entrepreneurs, is also used in workshops and in training programs of many universities.

My way of doing business can be summarized as **Converting Idle Capacity Into Cash**®, which has been examined by many academicians and featured in internationally refereed professional journals in management; it is referred to as the Altuntas Formula by academic researchers. I am very happy to be not just a real role model for entrepreneurs but also a source of inspiration for academicians to study and discover unique and beneficial methods for entrepreneurs.

In my opinion, the journey to entrepreneurship is like the four seasons of the year. The first season is the level of wannapreneurship. The second season is the stage of starting up a business. This stage has three important sub-steps: innovation, entrepreneurship, and marketing and sales. The third season is the growth stage. This stage includes branding, institutionalization, and franchising. Lastly, the fourth season is the maturity stage: leadership and angel investment.

## Before Starting Up the Business

## Step 1: Wannapreneurship

This is the process that starts the moment that you produce a business idea. But how will you proceed from this wannapreneurship stage to the next level? Are you a wannapreneur? Inventor? Entrepreneur? Why could Edison, one of the world's most important inventors, not manage to be successful as an entrepreneur in his businesses?

I was told by everybody around me, "You cannot do it;" or "You cannot succeed;" or "Only you could come up with such an idea." But I succeeded in collecting $100,000 in a month with an idea that nobody quite understood. You have to read my story with Azmi Saribay to understand how I realized the transition from wannapreneurship to entrepreneurship.

First, I developed a business idea based on observations while I was working at the travel agency. I wanted to take a training course on tour operating, but I couldn't find one. When I found, via my network, the opportunity to use the idle capacity of a physical facility, I developed a business model that I would first earn and then spend. I had to develop this kind of system because I had just $400, which is virtually nothing for starting up a business.

I implemented my business model. I spent my $400 on an advertisement, and I realized a return of $100,000 on that investment at the end of the following month. So I generated my financing from the business model I produced.

Now, please write similar stories you have for this step and answer the following questions in your story:

- How did you find your business idea?
- What did people say about your business idea?
- What sort of a business model did you develop in your head?
- What kind of opportunity did you seize? Why was there a certain need for your product or service?

## Starting Up the Business

## Step 2: Innovation

You have to develop a product or a service or a unique marketing strategy that your competitors in the market haven't thought of before. If you innovate, you can freely spend for marketing. If you haven't developed something innovative and are simply doing what other entrepreneurs are doing, you are carrying a serious risk. You are spending your money to promote a product that doesn't have an innovative feature, yet it is the same price as branded products; as a result, the consumer remembers he needs this product and purchases the branded product. If you had developed an innovative product or had assigned an innovative feature to an existing product, the consumer would say, "Let me try this!"

I developed one totally new service for the market and assigned two completely new innovations to the service I offered.

In the educational market, only foreign language and computer courses were available. My plan was to develop totally new vocational training programs for the first time in the market: tour operator courses, passenger fares and ticketing courses, flight attendant courses, airport passenger services courses, human resource management courses, airline management courses, and public relations courses. Consumers needed help in finding a job when they completed my innovative courses, so I looked for ways to facilitate recruitment for travel agencies, airlines, and other companies. I understood there was a need for a job-placement service and for cooperation with national and international authorities for certifying participants, which would also facilitate graduate's job placement. Because job placement is crucial to sustaining the business, I decided to focus on this area.

Years later, while I was a student at the university, I was recognized as one of the top forty innovative businessmen. My life story was filmed by the Turkish Radio and Television Corporation (TRT) and became a model throughout the country for innovative thinking.

Now, please write your own similar stories about this step and answer the following questions:

> • What innovative products or services have you developed?
> • What innovative features have you developed for your products or services?
> • In what way were they innovative?
> • Do the innovative features of your product or service match what you promise in your promotion message?

## Step 3: Entrepreneurship

Now it is time to implement what you have dreamed with your right brain and planned with your left brain. The world always welcomes a new entrepreneur. The moment you receive your identification tax number is the beginning of your entrepreneurship story. You were a wannapreneur, but now you're a full entrepreneur. This is the time to concentrate on becoming a *successful* entrepreneur.

I implemented the business model I developed, which consists of innovative features as described above. I rented an office in the main business district of the city that was easily accessible to all my potential customers. I made sure the small office provided a welcoming environment where customers would feel comfortable as soon as they walked through the door. I devised a name for my business that would sound international, reliable, respectable and that had potential for becoming an international brand name. The word *Deulcom* had no meaning on its own, but everybody perceived it as a reliable, respectable, international company. I found a secretary with excellent telephone skills and who knew how to make sure customers felt they were important to us.

My entrepreneurship story started by bringing together an innovative business idea, trust in myself, the correct office location, a convincing company name, and the right kind of staff. My next step was to determine correct and affordable prices for the consumer and develop a suitable business model that would generate business without large outlays of cash. I defined my vision for my newly established business: Deulcom would be an internationally recognized brand in the educational market.

While making the decision to pour all the money I had into an advertisement, the question I asked myself was simply, *What would I risk losing, and how would I replace that amount in case it didn't work out?* When I made my calculation, I wouldn't lose too much, but I had an opportunity of making so much more. That was my moment of decision.

I set up the first job-placement center in the country. Then I made agreements with national and international certification bodies, such as IATA and Bosphorus University, that would facilitate placement for my course graduates.

Now, please write your similar stories about this step and answer the following questions:

- Did you find the correct office address?
- Does your company name have the potential to become an international brand?
- Did you determine the correct price for your products or services?
- Do you trust yourself in implementing all the things you had in mind?
- Did you have a Plan B if you didn't succeed?
- What is your vision for your new start-up? What is your target in the future?
- How did you implement your innovative business model?

## Step 4: Marketing and Sales

How will you succeed in becoming a leader in business with a minimum budget but maximum sales records? That is a big challenge for entrepreneurs. I have learned that entrepreneurs are very careful about spending money for marketing and that successful entrepreneurs are the ones who are personally involved with marketing planning and activities.

Spending great sums for marketing doesn't guarantee great sales. Spending for *correct* marketing tools is a smarter way of running marketing campaigns, whereas you can generate maximum sales with minimum budgets.

I discovered a very interesting page in the daily papers on which to advertise my courses. Since my courses were for people who were looking for jobs and were therefore looking at the job vacancy pages, I placed my advertisements on the job-vacancy page, which was considerably less expensive than the other pages. In this way, I was able to reach my potential customers by spending less than I would have otherwise. Deulcom was also the first educational training company cooperating with a professional advertising agency. That was an innovation for the educational sector in those times.

I succeeded in making $100,000 with an advertisement that cost me $400. In the following years, I became the sector leader with an annual marketing budget of $10 million.

I started my university life taking buses between home and the campus, but eighteen months after placing my first advertisement, I had my own BMW and a chauffeur to drive me around. That illustrates the real impact of good marketing decisions.

I also have to underline the importance of sales skills. Yes, you can bring customers into the office by smart marketing strategies, but that doesn't guarantee sales.

It is like a football game. Ten players are bringing the ball to the nearest goalpost, but if the team doesn't have a good forward, they cannot win. By the same token, if you don't have a good sales staff, what you spend for marketing will be for nothing.

I first began selling courses myself, and then I taught my staff how to sell. My office was next the sales office, so it was easy for me to listen in on the sales presentations.

If the entrepreneur succeeds in selling, he will progress. If he doesn't succeed in selling, he will have to go back, find another business idea, and follow the same steps. Marketing and sales is the second milestone for an entrepreneur. The first was your decision to set up your business.

Now, please write your stories about this step and answer the following questions:

- What marketing strategies did you develop?
- Have you found innovative ways of marketing?
- How did you develop your sales team?
- What was your Plan B if you consumed all your money for marketing, yet couldn't realize the target sales?

## Growing the Business

## Step 5: Branding

By spending money for marketing, be aware that you are killing two birds with one stone. You are creating your customer and you are also informing the customer about your brand by using the emblem, logo, and slogan on your advertisements and other marketing tools. Over time, your emblem and logo can become highly recognizable in your market. It starts to be a reason for customers to choose your product over others. The more the customer sees your trademark in his daily life (newspapers, magazines, billboards, the Internet, and so on), your trademark becomes a very valuable brand for the market.

Paying close attention to the branding process is therefore essential. Becoming an entrepreneur who owns a well-known brand means that you have a serious responsibility on your shoulders. You should concentrate on the quality of the product or your service more than ever. At the beginning of the game, you were a fresh entrepreneur, and the customer was aware of that. The customer was forgiving of your mistakes. But when you own a brand, the customers don't buy products because they believe in the marketing messages alone; they consume the product or service primarily because they trust the brand.

So, at the beginning of the entrepreneurship journey, the entrepreneur comes first, but later, it is the brand that comes first. For an entrepreneur who owns a well-known brand, taking new steps is a must: institutionalization and franchising are the natural next steps to branding.

While I was having ads prepared for newspapers, magazines, and billboards, I was spending more time at the advertising agency than at my office. I was like a staff member. I discovered I had a good eye for visual impact and was using this skill for my own company. I was invoiced by the agency for half of the normal amount because I was there working for them.

Deulcom became one of the fastest growing brands of Europe and was honored by Eurowards. The award ceremony was the first time I had been introduced as the owner of one of the best-known brands in the country. The interesting side of this was that I was still a student at the university.

To come to that level, I was spending millions of dollars on advertising in the early 1990s, and this money would return to me. I will show you how that money came back to me in the following steps.

Now, please answer the following questions to see if you are on the right road toward branding:

- Do you use advertising agencies or develop your own ads?
- Are you aware that your goal should be to create your brand at the same time you are selling your products and services?
- What methods did you develop to accelerate your branding process?
- Do you own a brand? What does your brand say to the customer?
- Do you agree that one of the most important objectives of a successful entrepreneur is to create a well-known brand?
- In your opinion, which is more difficult: creating a brand or maintaining the prestige of the brand you created?

## Step 6: Institutionalization

Your business grows up and you have many branches now. This growing-up comes with not a few headaches. New staff, new branch offices, more reporting, more work on daily operations, more customers. All these bring new challenges, and entrepreneurs need to find effective solutions.

I tried to handle all these issues of ten branches all over the country and more than five hundred staff when I was just twenty-six years old. While branding was going on and every day new customers were taking advantage of Deulcom's services, my company was becoming the top company in that particular sector, where everybody wanted to work. Every day, I was receiving hundreds of e-mails from people who wanted to work at one of Deulcom's branches. The second most desirable place to work was the British Council.[14] All that happened in five years as a result of innovations, relevant, and carefully thought-out marketing plans and strong management of the branding process.

When you come to that stage, you understand that the customer gives importance to delivery style and the quality of service or products. He realizes that what he pays includes quality management of the services and the quality of financial services made available to him, in addition to the quality of the service or product itself. I observed that customer complaints were rarely related to the quality of the English language lessons they bought. They were about the late delivery of certificates, the drinks sold at the canteen, a missed SMS reminder about tuition payment dates, and so on.

Then I started studying management by reading books and articles and participating in conferences and seminars. In a short time, I understood that my company needed to have four departments:

1. Management and Organization
2. Product Management
3. Marketing and Sales Management
4. Accounting and Financial Management

Someone should be responsible for **management and organization**. Human resources management was 90 percent of the management and organization, especially in the service sector. This person would act as the CEO and would be responsible for the smooth running of the other three departments.

Another person should be responsible for **product management.** Because Deulcom was a training company, product management meant training management. Training management required a person with experience in the educational operations of a school or a university. For example, recruiting the head of the foreign languages department of a university was an excellent solution.

Someone should be responsible for the **marketing and sales department.** This person should ideally have a background in sales, someone who can also achieve a balance and cooperation between the marketing team in the office and the sales team in the field. This person should also be able to teach and coach others. Each salesperson needs both sales and product training, and the head of marketing was responsible for delivering this training.

Someone should be responsible for **accounting and financial management.** I had to hire new accounting staff, because new branches meant more customers, and this meant much more work on daily operations. Cash-flow management and cost management also required new staff. I also had to make agreements with independent auditing firms for accounting and financial consulting and the legally required financial reports.

I was responsible for all those four departments as an entrepreneur, but five Deulcom branches with 250 staff made it impossible to follow the day-to-day operation of every department. It was at that point that I pressed the institutionalization button.

First, I decided in what capacity I could best serve the interests of Deulcom. I decided I had to be both CEO and marketing and sales manager by virtue of my extensive experience and strong ability in this area. The status of the general manager, who had been acting in the capacity of a CEO, was changed to board member status, thus opening enough space for myself at the headquarters. I recruited an HR manager, who would assist in recruiting new staff and follow up on the existing staff. I recruited the head of the foreign languages department of a university as the training manager responsible for the quality of instruction in the classrooms. His only concern would be how we could improve the quality of instruction for our course participants. I made an agreement with a good auditing firm that would report directly to me every month about the company's financial situation.

This institutionalization process took approximately eighteen months, by which time I had a 500-page company manual in my hand.

It included all details on procedures, even down to the level of how birthdays would be celebrated in the company. Daily operational objectives were included as well, and this book was adopted by a university professor in 1999 for his course in total quality management.

Now, please answer the following questions to see if you have completed your institutionalization step:

- Do you offer to the customer a service or a product?
- How do you control the daily operations of your company? What kind of system did you develop for delivering the services and products to the customer?
- Did you feel that you didn't have time at the company for developing new systems because you were spending all your time with daily operation details?
- What is the organizational structure of your company?
- Who is responsible for the management and organization of your company?
- Who is responsible for product or service quality?
- Who is responsible for marketing and sales?
- Who is responsible for accounting and finance?
- What do you excel in? Marketing and sales? Accounting and finance? HR management? Management and organization? Product management?
- Do you believe that what the customer pays is for the product only? Or does what he pays for also include the pre-sales, during sales, and after-sales quality?

## Step 7: Franchising

Following your branding process, independent entrepreneurs start requesting your brand for their own use. This is where the franchising process starts. What you have to pay attention to at this stage is that other entrepreneurs who want to get your franchise may assume that you have completed your institutionalization process. It is not always obvious to would-be-franchisees whether you have completed this process or not, because they are not inside the company. They simply see your advertisements regularly, probably consume your services and products and enjoy them, and see that you have so many customers, and they therefore decide to purchase your franchise. But all this does not necessarily mean you are ready to franchise your business. The essential criterion is whether you have completed the institutionalization process and have a manual for daily operations. Are you ready to franchise your business?

Franchising means more than just letting your brand be used by other entrepreneurs. Franchising includes transfer of know-how. You have to share all the secrets of your business in a very structured way. The franchisee is paying not only for the brand but also for the know-how of making the business succeed.

I was very lucky because, before setting up my business, I had learned the principles of franchising during the years I was on the board of the Turkish Franchising Association. I observed how new US brands were coming to Turkey and what sort of interviews they were conducting with potential franchisees. I tried to understand how they were choosing the best possible entrepreneurs who would run the business. That was a great experience for me, and I decided that if one day in the future, I owned my own company, I would concentrate on franchising my business. I learned, among other things, that one key element is the manual to teach the franchisee how to run the business successfully. For that reason, I spent a lot of time writing all my business procedures into the manual.

I advise you to have a very clear vision for the future of your business. You should be amassing franchisees in the future, and if you establish a clear goal from the beginning, you know why you should give importance to marketing strategies, branding, and the institutionalization process. As a matter of fact, **a franchising system is a way of getting a good return on the investment you made for branding and institutionalization**. If you don't establish a goal that includes franchising for your business, you will spend more time and more money to do it when you eventually decide to franchise.

When I had ten branch offices and more than 500 staff at Deulcom and had completed the manual, I started conducting interviews with potential franchisees. I didn't announce that I would give franchises to entrepreneurs, but I had a long list of entrepreneurs who wanted to set up new Deulcoms in their cities; I sent each one an e-mail to see if they were still interested.

Once I started franchising Deulcom, an international investment group made a proposal to me. They wanted to operate a Spanish language school in Turkey, and instead of losing time creating a new brand for the Turkish market, they wanted to run their business under the Deulcom brand. We agreed on a franchise fee of 150,000 Euro for a five-year term, and the next morning, one of my Deulcom branches became a franchise that was owned by Spanish investors. This particular franchise fee was one of the highest among the national and international brands franchised in Turkey.

That was a valuable experience for me. Inspired by the franchise agreement I made with the Spanish investors, I developed a wider range of options for potential entrepreneurs. By that time, I was the owner of one of the country's most valuable trademarks; all my schools are now run by independent entrepreneurs.

Over time, I developed new brands that derived from the original Deulcom brand, each with different investment schemes and each with a different entrepreneur profile:

- Deulcom International: vocational training school
- Deulcom Institute: foreign language school
- Deulcom Kids: child care up to the age of six; this carries an entrepreneurship lab, which is very attractive for women entrepreneurs
- Deulcom Abroad: registration offices for those who want to study abroad

I was very pleased to read an article in the monthly economy magazine *Capital* describing me as "the father of franchising in Turkey" and showing me as a business role model. The most motivating side of the franchising system is that you are dealing with entrepreneurs like yourself, which creates a great synergy. That is, from my personal perspective, more enjoyable and significant than what you charge as franchise fee.

Now you have to answer the following questions to see if you are ready to franchise your business.

> - Are you receiving e-mails from independent entrepreneurs wanting to make a franchise agreement with you?
> - Is your company manual ready?
> - Have you developed the ability to identify the correct entrepreneurs?
> - Are you aware that you will have to include teaching franchisees how to run the business in your business objectives?
> - Have you developed a system to monitor the performance of your franchisee?
> - Have you developed a franchise agreement that matches the legal requirements of your country?

## Maturing the Business

## Step 8: Leadership

You can carry on as the CEO of your company, or you can replace yourself with a professional CEO, which will free you to become the leader of your business. Which is the right path for you?

After I started franchising, I eventually had seventeen schools, each of which was owned by a different entrepreneur. They are now paying 10 percent of their revenues every month as royalty, with a minimum 1,500 Euro payment, and paying a minimum of 35,000 Euros every five years as a franchise fee. Now I have only five staff at the Deulcom Headquarters responsible for daily operations of franchises such as preparation of exams, organizing marketing budgets, certifying graduates, and making pre-interviews of new franchise applications.

I appointed my wife, Rakibe, as the CEO of Deulcom, so I am no longer in the Deulcom game as an active daily player. Instead, I am leading Deulcom, which is something quite different from playing in the field. I preferred to lead Deulcom twenty years after I started this business from scratch.

What am I doing, as the leader of Deulcom, for the benefit of the Deulcom brand and its franchisees? I am actually working in the capacity of a business development manager, developing innovative courses for franchisees and making agreements with national and international bodies. Those agreements are not just increasing the sales of my franchisees but also increasing the value of the Deulcom brand.

In addition, I am organizing receptions and monthly meetings, as well as giving interviews to the media and speeches at national and international conferences about the importance of certified staff in developing economies. I am supporting my franchisees by my presence at every possible conference, exhibition, and fair as the president of Deulcom's executive committee, which comprises representatives of franchises.

What advantage did I gain in passing to the leadership stage? The most important advantage is the time I now have for myself, which makes it possible for me to write books for new entrepreneurs, give speeches on entrepreneurship, write weekly columns for economy magazines, and participate in TV shows like *Dragons' Den*.

**With financial and time independence at the age of forty, I am now able to use my time as I please.**

My book became a bestseller in Turkey, and its sales surpassed those of the book by Steve Jobs,[15] who inspired hundreds of thousands of people all over the world. I became the ambassador of the World Entrepreneurship Forum to Turkey and the Balkan countries, and I now foster the business ecosystem of those countries. I am able spend time and energy for other people. Social entrepreneurship projects, such as choosing twenty university students from twenty different countries every year and teaching them how to make money from scratch by assigning them specific tasks, to let them learn by doing, is my favorite social project. It may be unique in the world. I am awarding the winners each year with internship opportunities to help them develop their entrepreneurial skills in different countries, and I fund the entire experience.

If I hadn't left my chair to a new CEO of Deulcom, I would have had no time for doing something new and different in the world. Please don't forget that leadership is not a position in a company; my business card doesn't identify me as "leader." Leadership is a mindset that directs your life activities toward making the world a better place for yourself and others. What you received from the world is an index of your financial success. **The amount of money you make can be one criterion for defining success, but once you have made your fortune, it is time to redefine success in terms of what you give to the world.** The more you give, the more successful you are.

You also have to decide at this step whether it is worth working so much to become a millionaire if it also means that you never see your children grow up. So now, please answer the following questions to see if you are a candidate to become your life's leader.

- Is your business in a position where you can turn over CEO duties to another professional?
- Do you enjoy being active in social projects?
- Do you enjoy dedicating your time and energy and money to talented young people who can be good entrepreneurs in the future?
- Why did you make money? To let it lead your life? Or to enable you to lead your own life?
- How will you use your entrepreneurial skills to further develop your company when you are not in the game?

## Step 9: Angel Investment

You spent years completing the first eight stages I've described. Now is time to support new start-up entrepreneurs. You should enable them by sharing your know-how. An angel investor is the experienced entrepreneur who has learned all the ropes and is now ready to provide financial support, know-how, and networking for new entrepreneurs by becoming shareholders in their company. How do you become an angel investor? How can entrepreneurs access the financial opportunities that angel investors can provide? How can entrepreneurs take a seat at Silicon Valley?

I became an angel investor after becoming a dragon at the *Dragons' Den*. Becoming a Dragon also required a time commitment in addition to personal wealth, and thanks to my status in life, I was able to give time and make investments in the context of that program.

Following the show, I started listening to business ideas every day and everywhere I went. One day on my way to the airport, I had just stopped at a red light when a police car appeared with its alarm blaring and directed me to pull over. I had no idea what I had done wrong. Then two police officers approached me and explained they were watching *Dragons' Den* every Friday night; they had a business idea and wanted to know if I had time to listen to it. I had to get to airport rather quickly, but I gave them my card so that they could e-mail me their business idea later.

Every day, I receive approximately fifty e-mails from all over the world, and I have set up a team to screen the written pitches of entrepreneurs. As an angel investor, you are now able to dedicate your know-how, network, and money for high-growth start-ups. In this way, one of your feet is always at the first step of the entrepreneurial journey and trying to take all those steps with a fresh entrepreneur.

What did I do to develop my angel-investment skill? I first ordered ten books on angel investment from Amazon and studied them like a university student. I really became an expert of this system, because I understood easily owing to my experience with making angel investments in the studio. I am not sure if all Dragons have such expertise in the angel-investment system, but I developed my own knowledge so that I could to teach it even in international workshops of EBAN, the European Business Angels Network.

I advise you to study the system by participating in any workshop you find in your country. If none are available in your country, register for EBAN Institute trainings in Europe. These take place twice a year. The Angel Capital Association (ACA) in the United States also offers similar training.

Now, please answer the following questions to see if you are ready to become an angel investor:

- Do you have the time, the network, and the wealth to become an angel investor?
- Do you enjoy working with entrepreneurs?
- Do you have sufficient resources such as time, a wide network, and capital? Have you developed angel-investment skills, such as the following?
  - Screening the deal and conducting due diligence
  - Negotiating and forming the legal contracts
  - Monitoring the investment
  - Exiting the investment
  - Valuing the start-up

# 13

## Tried-and-True Techniques from the Voice of Experience

G et ready now: I have decided to share with you the business model I developed for my daughters, a one-of-a-kind business model for entrepreneurs. This is the enhanced model of my company from the days I first built it. I only need super salespeople who are extremely honest! All you need to do is to partner up with a friend and take on a budget of $400 dollars per entrepreneur per month, just like my daughters will.

I am sure that you, as someone with an entrepreneurial spirit, have been thinking of starting and developing your own business one day.

Most new entrepreneurs find financing a major concern. I am aware that a good number of people, although they believe they have entrepreneurial skills, find out they need serious help in starting their own business. I also know that, even though some entrepreneurs are able to find financing, their business may fail because of lack of expertise.

Over time, I have learned that if entrepreneurs have the right skills for business—that is, if they are hard-working, have good sales ability, and enjoy teamwork—they can produce wonders when given opportunities like financing and mentorship, even with very little capital.

\* \* \*

As my daughters grow up, I want to include them in my business, but there are nagging questions at the back of my mind: Are they as skillful as me? Are they inclined toward entrepreneurship? How successful are they in human relations? How do they react under stress? Can they deal with bureaucracy? Do they have a flair for sales?

When you take a look at their school grades, it looks as if they could well achieve even more success than I have. Unfortunately, however, school grades do not reflect any of the characteristics described above. In order to test my daughters, I have decided to create an atmosphere similar to the one that led me into the business world years ago. I have developed a business model to help them enter the entrepreneurial world that allows me to watch over them for twelve months.

Here is the framework:

- They will have to locate a small office for a training center, 100-150 square meters, just like when I started.
- They will get a personal loan from a bank, with a maximum monthly payment of $800, which they will be paying themselves.
- I am going to supply mentoring.

My daughters will be making their payments to the bank, $400 each. This will encourage discipline in making regular repayments in a timely manner. I will not help them at all with their payments, because I know that they raise the money by teaching fifteen private lessons per month. The risk they are taking is therefore not terribly substantial; it can easily be dealt with.

If they implement the business plan correctly and demonstrate sales ability, they can feasibly make a $25,000 profit even in the first year of their business. This is the same mentality I built my company with.

I will, in this way, learn how well my daughters are likely to deal with sales and bureaucracies. They will learn how entrepreneurial they really are. With this project, I am killing two birds with one stone: they will get to know themselves, and I will get to know their abilities. There will be no money paid on my part and, on top of it all, if they succeed, they will make money!

If, at the end of twelve months, they come to me and say, "Dad, these classrooms are not enough for us anymore; we need a bigger place," we have a win-win situation.

\* \* \*

While planning all this, I came to the realization that the business model I developed for my daughters actually addressed a need of other many other entrepreneurs as well. Why shouldn't two English teachers, or a retired bank manager, or three new graduates, or two retired flight attendants get together to start a business with an investment of $400 each and aim for $25,000 profit each year?

## I Invite You to be a Wise Entrepreneur

Wise entrepreneurs take calculated risks, do not spend all their money at once, are patient, and learn the business before expanding it. They earn first, and then they spend!

My own strategy, which made me the entrepreneur I am today, is to earn first, spend later. The new business model I developed for my daughters takes this principle as its foundation. Maximum profit with minimum investment. A wise entrepreneur has to figure this first: If I cannot succeed, will this risk be turning my life upside down and cause me to lose all my savings?

## Be Careful When Building Your Business

The risks you are taking should not turn your life upside down if things go wrong. Your risk is $800 if you are an individual entrepreneur, $400 in the case of two, and only a little over $250 if you have two partners. These figures will never put you at risk of turning your life upside down. This amount is one that you can easily pay by working somewhere else and making that money again. You have to realize a model where you will earn first and then collect to pay off your expenses. This concept forms the basis of the new business model for my daughters. It becomes a self-financing system with a six-month grace period and is the kind of investment for which you can easily get financing from your friends and family or from a bank—so long as you have an ability to sell!

You have to focus on sales! You should not waste time with operations such as the daily business flow, preparation of catalogs, exams, certificates, personnel allocation, determining textbooks, Google ads, development and maintenance of a website, preparation of the marketing plan, course scheduling, etc. Let all these be handled by others, and you handle the sales, sales, and more sales.

Once you build your business, you should be able to expand as soon as you reach your capacity. I named this new business model The Deulcom Institute Model, and it takes the successful entrepreneur to new levels within twelve months. If you are a really good entrepreneur, within twelve months, your classroom capacity will be filled and you will need to expand. In this case, the entire infrastructure needed is ready, as long as you sell, sell, sell.

## The Deulcom Institute Business Model

Unemployment is one of the biggest problems the world faces today; yet, everyone is looking for qualified personnel.

Right at this point is where entrepreneurs like you are needed. Your basic project should be to train qualified personnel who know English, who are equipped with vocational skills, and whose certification is recognized both nationally and internationally. When you sign up for a Deulcom Institute, you are signing yourself up for success in a social enterprise, along with having made a wise entrepreneurial move. The training sector offers good rewards, both social and commercial. You just need to know how to take advantage of them. The Deulcom Institute business model leaves entrepreneurs in control of their sales and marketing activities. All the management and organization, product management, and accounting are handled by the Deulcom headquarters so as to relax the entrepreneur and keep motivation high.

## Always Build Your Business with Minimum Financing

Funding is a major challenge for entrepreneurs. Financing is not really that hard if you have a viable business idea. You can combine several instruments from the list below. For example, you can secure partial financing from friends and family, and get the rest as a personal loan from the bank; or vendors may offer special payment terms.

### Your Own Capital

You can use your own capital. My advice, however, is to keep your equity as a reserve and instead, secure that amount as bank credit. This way, you will be able to conduct business without having financing difficulties for a specified period. Once you start managing your business, the rest gets easier.

### Vendor Payment Term Opportunities

Some vendors may offer up to twenty-four months' credit on sales. They may also offer their own financing for purchase of their products.

### Friends and Family

You can get support from your friends and family to set up your own business. Keep in mind that this is generally one of the least risky methods of financing.

### Credit Cards

You can use your credit cards, especially during promotional campaigns and by taking advantage of deferred payment plans, thus avoiding interest payments.

## Personal Loans

You can secure low-interest personal loans from banks for your company's start-up investment capital. Banks also sometimes offer special plans with a six-month deferred payment clause.

## Franchising Credit

If banks offer, for instance, a sixty-month franchising loan package with a six-month deferred payment option for your business, you will need to make monthly payments of $800 for fifty-four months for a loan of $25,000 after the six-month deferral. By doing so, you are implementing the "first make money, then pay back the loans" business model.

## Basket System

You can mix and match any or all of the above options, with the percentage of each depending on your individual needs and resources.

### Now Ask Yourself These Two Very Important Questions:

1. Are you a good salesperson?
2. Does it excite you to think of owning your own business?

If you have answered yes to both questions, if you would like to be an entrepreneur via a Deulcom Institute in your country, and if you would like to be my business partner, all you have to do is send me your resume: baltuntas@deulcom.com.tr

# 14

# Lessons for Future Entrepreneurs

Everyone should constantly strive to improve him- or herself. It's difficult to forget the positive role models you had early in life. In this chapter, I share with you true stories that provide examples from real situations to help show you the way to improvement.

## Not Everyone Has to be an Entrepreneur

You may remember the story of the magic stone from my elementary school days. Fast forward: Serdar passed the entrance exam for a private high school, while I started at a public school. My family was encouraging me to learn foreign languages, so on the weekends, I attended English courses. Even though he was in a yearlong intensive English program at his private school, Serdar also attended these courses. Once again, we found ourselves in the same classroom on the weekends.

Back then, pen pals were a very popular way of practicing one's English. I found fifteen pen pals by paying ten dollars to an organization and then sold them for a total of one hundred dollars to my friends who had not been able to find pen pals for themselves. Serdar was among the buyers. Let me direct your attention to the fact that I was always providing the supply and Serdar was always providing the demand. He was always a customer. I gave Serdar's English studies a lot of support by providing him with an English-speaking pen pal.

Time passed, we graduated, and we both got into the prestigious Bosphorus University. Serdar studied civil engineering, and I was in the Foreign Language Education Department. Our paths crossed once again. As I have explained earlier, when I wasn't going to my classes at the university, I was working at a travel agency. Serdar was learning to play the guitar.

"Baybars," he said one day, "you probably have customers at the travel agency coming from Bulgaria. Do you think it would be possible to have one of them bring me a guitar from there? They're a lot cheaper there."

"My pleasure," I said. I helped him buy the guitar by supplying both the guitar and the foreign currency.

I am actually describing the story of two students—me and Serdar—with similar family and educational backgrounds. The roles of these two people remained the same, with one always selling something, and the other always buying. It might be a magic stone, an address, or a guitar—or anything else, for that matter.

What happened as a result? I graduated from the Foreign Language Education Department and became an entrepreneur. Serdar graduated in civil engineering and became a guitarist. My advice is that we have to do what makes us happy and what we excel in, as we have only one life to live. I know that Serdar enjoys what he is doing as much as I enjoy what I do. What you get materially is transient. We need to bear this in mind and push aside the passion of earning money. I never took the road for making money (although I did make money), I went to where my heart took me, and after all, what did I have to lose?

## What I Learned from One of Forbes's Top 100 Businessmen

Mr. Vitali Hakko, who was on the Forbes list of the top one hundred businessmen of Turkey, founded the Beyoglu Heritage Association and developed it into one of the most renowned associations in Turkey, which took important steps toward making Beyoglu an important center for business and the arts. One day, he gave a speech to the association. He was ninety years old at the time and had recently been discharged from the hospital, still with a lingering a fever. He was having a hard time walking, even with help. Despite his situation, he spoke for an hour, describing Beyoglu's future. I will never forget that day. To make a long story short, some entrepreneurs were wondering how much longer he was going to keep working. I remember his speech providing the answer: "... until the end of my days!"

We lost Mr. Hakko about six months after that speech. He was an entrepreneur until the moment he breathed his last breath.

* * *

One day, I was on the phone with Mr. Hakko when he suddenly cried out, "Ahhhh!" "What's wrong?" I asked, thinking that something really bad had happened. He replied calmly that his nurse was giving him a shot while he was talking to me about Beyoglu. His spirit of entrepreneurship did not recognize age, illness, or treatments.

If you are an entrepreneur at seven, you are still an entrepreneur at seventy. It is as if it is embedded in your DNA. This sometimes works along with commercial entrepreneurship, sometimes with social entrepreneurship. But these are two different areas.

Vitali Hakko had already built a hugely successful business and developed it to a point where it could operate independently, but he did not want to take a backseat in life. In other words, while he was sitting in the technical director's seat, he still wanted to be in the ball game. He continued entrepreneurial activities, but in a different area. Since he did not want to interfere in an existing system that functioned well, he turned his attention to social issues.

The Beyoglu Heritage Association was Vitali Hakko's social arena. Like Mr. Hakko, I founded and managed many associations, and I am currently the president of the Business Angels Association in Turkey. And like Mr. Hakko, I eventually channeled my entrepreneurial skills to social issues. I have found that success in social projects actually gives me more satisfaction than my commercial successes. I therefore encourage successful entrepreneurs to enter both areas.

## Do Not Tell the Media More Than What They Need to Know

One day, during the time when I was the president of Beyoglu Heritage Association, a journalist called me. She needed to interview a certain famous person's father, who reportedly lived in Beyoglu, and she needed my help to find out where she could locate this person. Mr. Hakko's cousin would surely know the answer, I thought.

Putting the journalist on hold, I had my assistant connect me to Mr. Hakko's cousin. In the meantime, the journalist continued her chat with me.

At that time, there was a serious pickpocketing problem on Istiklal Avenue in Beyoglu that we had not been able to curb. I wondered aloud if perhaps we might have fewer pickpocketing incidents if the street, then for pedestrians only, was to be open to traffic.

This was the extent of our conversation. The next day's newspaper announced: "The Beyoglu Heritage Association president is rebelling! Istiklal Avenue should be open to traffic to prevent pickpocketing." This was the supposed news. Our personal chat had made the news; yet I had made no such declaration. I couldn't even imagine that a personal conversation would be reported to the public—and inaccurately, at that!

The Beyoglu shopkeepers were irate. They accused the association of playing with their income. How could it be that they had no clue the street would be open to traffic? Why had they not been informed about this change? All hell broke loose. You need to be on your guard when talking to anyone from the press.

## Negotiating the Price from His Sickbed

We were aiming to renovate the pavement on Yesilcam Street, the Turkish film industry's equivalent of Hollywood Boulevard. We planned to carve into special stone the names and images of important people from the world of culture, art, politics, and business, starting with Vitali Hakko, who had contributed to the revival of Beyoglu's cultural-center status. The stones we wanted to use were manufactured using a special technique. We had a prototype made and learned that the cost was quite high, which meant we had to find a sponsor for this project.

The ideal sponsor was Vitali Hakko. Unfortunately, he had recently been hospitalized. Still, I felt compelled to show him the sample—and to engage him as a sponsor, so despite its very heavy weight, I carried the prototype to his hospital room to solicit his opinion. I anticipated he would probably agree to this project.

I started talking about the project, full of excitement and enthusiasm. I told him about the cost of the project and the sponsorship and that he would be the ideal candidate for sponsoring the project. Mr. Hakko suddenly sat up in his bed, completely revitalized. He found the cost too high.

He set his own price, what he figured was reasonable for his own pocket. *It is totally impossible to get it done for that much,* I thought to myself. Mr. Hakko's attitude constituted a good example of a true entrepreneur that day. A real entrepreneur can make financial analyses and decisions even in his sickbed.

All I could do was to wish him well and carry the heavy stone away.

## Trust Your Nose, Not Your Money

In order to sniff money, you have to know what it is to not have any. People who grew up and live around money cannot smell it, but people without a penny can.

An entrepreneur has to be good at smelling money. To a certain degree, I owe my present situation to this skill, which plays an important role in everything I do. People once asked Napoleon what it was that made him different from other people. He replied, "No difference, I am just able to think five minutes ahead of the others." This is exactly what I do: I think five minutes before most other people do and act immediately. It is that critical five minutes that can make the difference in achieving success.

If you do not have a target, you will not be running. You may not even be walking. An entrepreneur sets a target for himself and runs toward it.

When I first started university, I saw many of my friends driving luxury cars. I did not reprove or criticize them. I thought, *I can have that too if I try.* This is one of the "musts" of entrepreneurship. When you have money, you can make an investment, but when you don't have money and you still chase your business idea, this is entrepreneurship.

While you derive benefits for yourself, you also produce external benefits by setting up a business and employing personnel.

## I Established Ahmet Calik University without Ahmet Calik's Knowledge

Ahmet Calik is on the Forbes list of the top one thousand businessmen in the world and the owner of *Yeni Asir* (*New Century*), a major newspaper in the Aegean region. Its headquarters has a magnificent location in the middle of Izmir, adjacent to the Hilton Hotel. I thought to myself that this headquarters building should be utilized in a much better way, perhaps as a university building. It could become a city university, with a Faculty of Communications. The building belonged to the Calik Group, so they could also educate and train their own personnel in such an institution.

I wanted to convert the building into a university, but the building was not mine, and I didn't know Ahmet Calik. I had no connections with the Calik Group either. I was totally dreaming.

I found a friend who put me in touch with Ahmet Calik. Mr. Calik was very excited by my idea, and we made a deal. He would get 60 percent of the company, and I would found the university and get the other 40 percent.

He told me, "You are the right entrepreneur, and the idea is great, so let's discuss the location of the university later." He agreed, we shook hands, and theoretically, we established a company.

I understood that Mr. Calik was just my type of person. He does not hesitate to act when he sees a good opportunity. However, he was so busy with his other businesses that it was difficult for him to concentrate on new projects. The main articulation of the company that we were creating was prepared and waiting to be signed.

Time passed, but there was still no news from Mr. Calik; he was constantly abroad. We were able to talk over the phone on Sundays, but it was quite an accomplishment to reach him any other day!

The project wasn't making any progress and we were losing time, so I called our mutual friend to discuss the problem. He said, "October 27 is Turkmenistan's national day, and I am going to Turkmenistan, personally invited by the president. Mr. Calik will also probably come since he has investments there; you might be able to see and talk to him if you come along. It would be a nice surprise for him."

I agreed and together, we went to Turkmenistan for their national day.

We arrived at 6 a.m., and my travel companion received a VIP welcome. The welcoming committee wanted to take us to the presidential palace before the ceremony started at nine, but we were not allowed to leave the airport. The reason soon became apparent: in all that rush, I had forgotten to get a visa. Instead of sitting down with Ahmet Calik, I was about to get arrested! I was absolutely certain I was going to be arrested.

My friend was adamant that he would not leave without me. The police insisted they would send him to his hotel, with the promise of my joining him later. Their intent to arrest me was becoming even clearer to me.

The vice prime minister, who was among those who greeted us at the airport, finally called the minister of tourism, and my visa was issued at the airport upon his personal instructions.

Exactly at nine a.m., we were seated in the row just behind the president. I turned to my right side, and there was Ahmet Calik. "What are *you* doing here?" he said in astonishment.

I told him what happened and said, "I had to go through a lot of trouble to come here, so let's set up this company if you're ready." I had a very nice day with Ahmet Calik, and I met his entire team. We attended the national day celebrations.

I have not seen Ahmet Calik since then. I said to myself, *This is it. If he still cannot make a move after all this, there is no need for me to chase him.*

This illustrates how insistent an entrepreneur can be. Yet, it still bothers me that I could not do business with him. I quit chasing him. There is a good reason for everything.

## The Three Magic Numbers of the Entrepreneur: 7-24-365

I built my first business while I was a university student. I listen carefully when today's students come to me saying they have a business idea but no money. Since I had faced the same problem at their age, I always hear them out and offer advice. University students call me "the Dragon of university students" for that reason. I have received a lot of titles, but that one has been the most exciting one to date. I see all students as my friends. In the near future, they will move on to start their own businesses and become their own bosses. I take special pleasure from telling them about my own experiences.

7–24–365: Entrepreneurs have to love these numbers. Entrepreneurship recognizes no holiday, no vacation time, no business hours. When I have a new business idea, I work on it until I get it implemented. After I implement it, I work late into the night to get motivated to develop yet another new business idea. You have to get motivated again to develop a new business idea. This is a different kind of pleasure.

## The Benefits of Knowing Where to Stop

Mr. Kadir Topbas organized a meeting at city hall to receive well-wishers when he was first elected as the Istanbul Metropolitan Municipality mayor. He made a speech to the thousands of people who attended. I was among them, representing the Beyoglu Heritage Association. The former president of the association was also there. We wanted to congratulate the new mayor personally, but as soon as he finished his speech, the crowd closed in and he was completely surrounded. Chaos ensued.

There was no way we could approach him. We decided not to wait and made our way to the exit. On our way out, I noticed a security guard and stopped to ask him where the mayor was going to receive the guests.

"Sir," he said, "wait right where you are now." Indeed, the new mayor came in just a couple of minutes later, and I got to be the first person to congratulate him. You need to know or learn where to stand!

## I Opened My Eyes and Found Myself in the Hospital

I was only twenty-one years old when I started Deulcom, and at the beginning, I had only one secretary working for me. On top of it all,

I also opened a branch in another city, Izmir. I would take a plane to Izmir to enroll students, and then I would fly back to Istanbul to sell the programs to more students. I was making a lot of money, but I was working around the clock. I was talking to a hundred potential students a day. One day when I woke up, my tongue hurt when it touched my teeth! I ran to the mirror. My face was swollen, and I couldn't talk or eat. Panicked, I went to the hospital, and the doctor told me to stay in bed for a week. My immune system had collapsed, the biological harmony of the body had collapsed, and it attacked my mouth. It can show up in different parts of the body. I had found success, but this was how I ended up.

## Soup Houses Came to the Rescue of 7-Eleven

Entrepreneurship is very interesting. If you set your mind on something. You become an expert on all sorts of laws, rules, regulations, and obstacles and find a way to work around them.

The example for this is Mr. Ozer Ciller, the husband of the former prime minister of Turkey and the owner of all 7-Eleven shops in Turkey. He is among the most accomplished entrepreneurs I have ever met.

He brought 7-Eleven to Turkey. I was a student at the time and also the secretary-general of the Turkish Franchising Association, with Ozer Ciller as the president. 7-Eleven branches were opening all over the country, but there was a problem with the main one in Istanbul. 7-Eleven shops are, by definition, supposed to stay open twenty-four hours a day, which is the main concept. But the municipality regulations did not allow that. There is no point in operating a 7-Eleven if it has to close at night.

Municipality regulations, however, did allow soup eateries to stay open all night, and since 7-Eleven also sells soup, that was the way the problem was resolved. The first 7-Eleven in the world that accorded special significance to soup was in Istanbul.

When someone tells me something is against regulations, the 7-Eleven story immediately comes to mind. Entrepreneurs neither produce problems nor become a part of the problem. When they encounter an obstacle, they find a way to get around it!

## Coffee Cups from the United States for Fortune Tellers

One day, Mr. Ciller called me to his tiny office, much of which was filled with files and papers. I had envisioned a much bigger office. Mr. Ciller was very focused on his work; you couldn't even find a place in his room to sit down.

After a brief welcome, he took out a packaged set of Turkish-style coffee cups and handed them to me. "What are these for?" I asked. "I had these made when we were in the United States, with the intention of selling them to supermarkets." They come with a booklet that tells you how to read fortunes from the dregs of your Turkish coffee, in the way so many Turks know how to do. He hadn't had time to market them in the United States, so he brought them with him to Turkey, and now he was suggesting to me that I could sell them through supermarkets in this country!

I said, "Mr. Ciller, people in the United States may be curious about telling fortunes from coffee dregs, but here in Turkey, everyone knows how to do that, and besides, the instructions are all in English." Sensing my lack of interest, he put the box away. I understood: he is an entrepreneur who came up with this idea in the United States, had the sets made, but was not able to realize his plan. He is still looking to utilize it, unable to toss it out. He doesn't care if he makes any money out of it. He just wants the business idea to live and succeed.

## The Baybars Altuntas Rules

An entrepreneur has to have rules. If you are going to produce a product or service, you have to do it right. If this doesn't happen, and if what you sell is not good value for the money, this makes you something, but not an entrepreneur.

Laws, rules, and regulations may carry stipulations for the development of certain product types. However, even if it is not required by law, you are morally obligated to produce better quality if you can. For example, if there is a regulation that stipulates a paper product has to be ninety grams but it would be even better if you produce it at 300 grams, then it has to be 300 grams. In this way, you will be producing a quality brand, instead of simply buying and selling a product. Such individual decisions constitute the Baybars Altuntas rules.

I place a high value on my rules. One is to invest in good entrepreneurs. I am interested in the entrepreneur more than the project when making investments and entering into partnerships. Think of it this way: let's say an entrepreneur is the one who runs the ball down the field, and you are the coach. If your man in the field is good, he accepts the advice that you give, and if he applies his own ethical rules, then he is a good player. He may be a good player, but if he is not a successful one, then you have to change the game. For example, he might want to play basketball or soccer. He will not succeed if he does not have the skills of a soccer player, even if he insists. When a B-type of guy comes up with an A-type project—that is, a mismatch—I do not invest in him. I prefer to work with an A-type guy who comes to me with a B-type project.

## Be a People Collector

Entrepreneurs have to maintain their relationships well and be people collectors. I am a good people-collecting entrepreneur. Under normal conditions, for example, I might have thought, *This guy once laid me off, so I won't work with him ever again.* Yesterday has happened and is over and done with, so we have to look toward the future now. If something untoward happens as a result of a particular action, I take it as a lesson for the future. People-collecting is important. You can easily cross paths again with someone from your past but in an entirely different position. It is best to accept people first for who they are, and for what they do second.

Keep in mind the example of the general manager at the travel agency who laid me off but later ended up working for me. Remember the proverb: keep a thing for seven years and you will find a use for it.

## Listen to Everyone Politely, but Make Your Own Decision

Every time I visited Ozer Ciller he would greet me at the door—what a gentleman! This impressed me greatly from the very beginning, and I have taken his behavior as an example for myself.

Ozer Ciller was polite to everyone. He would listen to everyone, but he would do whatever he himself wanted to do. I adopted his positive approach toward each project and politeness as a model for myself. As I explained in an earlier chapter, although he would not say no to any project, at the end, he would do what he thought was best, having considered everyone's input. These behaviors made such a profound impression on me that I noticed at one point that I had started to see the glass half full. I would no longer think in negative terms. With this sort of mindset, it is actually very easy to win people's hearts.

## The Man Who Outsold Steve Jobs' Book

When I decided to write this book, everyone told me it was not the right time. "Why not?" I asked. Steve Jobs had just passed away. The whole media was buzzing with that news. His book had only recently been published. "No one will buy your book now; they will go for Jobs' book. His is the bestseller now in the business media."

I gave it some thought. I decided this would actually be the best time for publishing my own book. When the whole media was busy with Steve Jobs, and if there was no interest in my story, then I would have a good excuse if it didn't take off. I could just say, "Steve Jobs' book was just newly published and everyone was publishing news on that. There has been no interest in mine. Therefore, mine did not sell." And no matter what happened, everyone would see I was right. But if my book succeeded, that would be another story altogether. This would be a record high and my book would not be forgotten for at least a hundred years.

So I did not listen to people's advice and had this book published at, theoretically, the most inappropriate time. Steve Jobs had passed away on October 5, and his book was a bestseller. My book was first published on November 4 and was on the shelves the next week.

I believe it was within that first week that they called me very early one morning from the Anatolian Press Agency. "Congratulations, Mr. Altuntas. Your book has created a lot of resonance in the business world. As of last night, Steve Jobs' book dropped to second place on the bestseller list, with yours in first place! We would like to do an interview you."

I could not believe my ears. I checked the Internet immediately, and again, I could not believe my eyes! Never in my wildest dreams would I have believed something like this could happen. The book had been out only for a week, but it already surpassed Steve Jobs' book.

Once the Anatolian News Agency circulated the news, the whole media buzzed with headlines like, "The Man Who Outsold Steve Jobs' Book."

With my new title as the man whose book outsold the one by Steve Jobs, all the news media and almost all the TV channels started inviting me to do live interviews and talk programs. Within one month, I appeared on more than twenty TV programs.

Even after seven months, this book never dropped to second place, which put my signature on yet another record. Fortunately, everyone must have been wondering about how they could get off the bus and into a spercar!

Before the book appeared in the bookstores, I had asked an advertising agency to prepare a promotion campaign for the book. I immediately canceled my order. Right now, you are reading book that became a bestseller without a penny spent on advertising.

Within ten months, the book was in its twenty-second printing. Later, it was translated into Albanian and was on the shelves in Albania, Macedonia, Kosovo, Bosnia, and Herzegovina.

* * *

You see that I myself am following the entrepreneurship advice that I am offering you. If I had acted according to the advice other people gave me, you would not be reading this book now. I did listen but in the end did not heed their advice. Everybody knew me as a Dragon, but now they also knew me as a best-selling author. I have made a point to answer each and every e-mail I received from readers, and I developed a good relationship with them. We have become a very fine group.

## Baybars Altuntas Fan Club

One day, I was checking my Facebook page and found this message: "Anyone who would like to become a member of the Baybars Altuntas Fan Club should click here." I clicked. It was a fan page with five members.

I was not terribly concerned or even interested, to tell you the truth. I was not a singer or an artist. I was a businessman, an entrepreneur. No entrepreneur in the world had a fan club, so I figured this would not come to anything. One month passed, and the same message appeared again. This time, the fan club numbers had increased to almost 600.

This made me started taking it more seriously. Who were the founders of this club, and why did they start it? I sent an e-mail directly to the founder. I came across a follower of mine from a different city in Turkey. He had been closely following everything I was doing, so he had started this club to bring together people like himself. Then he became the club president.

Later on, I met them at a conference and over time our friendship developed. I had group that attended all my meetings and seminars. Eventually, the club had about 2,500 members that operate chapters in fifty cities, with each chapter having their own officers.

In March 2012, an introductory meeting was organized for all the fan club members in Istanbul. I attended with my younger daughter Eda. I met entrepreneurs from all over the country. The most interesting among them was a member of the German club, who came all the way from Germany. She later became the president of the German chapter of the fan club.

The club soon developed its own website. For the first time in the world, there was a fan club website for an entrepreneur, so I was really honored. You can also become members to the website at www. baybarsaltuntasfanclub.com

## Second Summit Organized in Turkey

You may recall my idea to have the second entrepreneurship summit in Turkey, following Obama's first Summit on Entrepreneurship in Washington, DC. With the support of the Turkish prime minister,

Turkey hosted the second Summit on Entrepreneurship December 3-4, 2011.

United States Vice President Joe Biden was present at the opening. The summit took place in Istanbul with a participation of three thousand entrepreneurs and ten ministers representing the government.

Joe Biden made a long speech, pointing to the importance of Turkish entrepreneurship for the world economy. The famous photograph picturing Obama and me was used in summit presentations and on various government websites.

This shows how important a business idea really is.

## The CNN International Studio in Washington, DC

"The founder of the Middle East Entrepreneurship Institute has arrived," said the attendant at the door as she checked my passport and announced my entry on the phone. We went upstairs, accompanied by two US executives who run PR for the Turkish embassy in Washington. In the car on the way to the studio, I had asked them several questions about live broadcasting. This was going to be my first time on a live broadcast completely in English. "Is there a chance we can get the questions beforehand?" I had asked.

The US executive replied, "We can ask once we get there, Mr. Altuntas." I reiterated the request in the elevator. After a while, he let me know me they had said that was not possible, but they could cancel my appearance on the program if I wanted to.

"No problem, let's continue," I replied.

I was in the studio. What is that? A minuscule studio, ten square meters at most. "Where's the interviewer?" I asked.

"The person asking the questions will be doing that from London. They'll give you earphones now, so you'll just listen to his questions and answer them as if he was here in the studio, while looking at this camera over there."

I could hear the question from across the Atlantic, but not all that clearly. The sound was very faint. When the program was over, I spoke to a former professor of mine in Turkey. It turned out he had seen the program. When he said, "You were superb!" I breathed a sigh of relief.

## Global Entrepreneurship Week

Every year in November, Global Entrepreneurship Week is celebrated around the world. The Turkish event for this special week was reported by *Milliyet* newspaper, one of the main dailies in the country.

> *Turkish entrepreneurs from all over the world met in Istanbul for an Entrepreneurship Forum as part of "Global Entrepreneurship Week," which is celebrated in 127 countries around the world. The focus of the week was Istanbul, but Manisa wasted no time this weekend, either.*
>
> *The Manisa Chamber of Commerce sponsored a session called "How to Become an Entrepreneur," presented by Baybars Altuntas, who so many young entrepreneurs were eager to meet. It was a pleasure to have met Mr. Altuntas and to be able to benefit from his ideas. He is a wonderful person, as well as his wife Rakibe.*
>
> *It would have been out of character with our traditional customs of hospitality not to treat our special guest, Mr. Altuntas, to a "sultan's tea" at the famous Ayni Ali Tea and Coffee House. So as soon as we collected him from the airport, that is exactly what we did. Thanks to Mr. Altuntas' wife, Rakibe, our conversation was videoed and posted on YouTube, which immediately generated comments from throughout the country. I even received messages on my cell phone.*
>
> *Once we had finished our "sultan's tea," it was time to make our way to the conference venue. The main conference room was filled to its 5,500-person capacity, with standing room only. Mr. Altuntas' speech was a great hit. We have learned the secrets of becoming an entrepreneur, and we have also taken clues from his last book.*[16]

\*\*\*

More than one hundred thousand people have attended my entrepreneurship conferences over the years in various countries. When I visit a country to present at a conference, I often see my photograph on billboards and advertisements. My audiences range in age from seven to seventy-seven, and participants include governors and mayors and other government officials. It's as if everyone aspires to be an entrepreneur! They all come wanting to learn my secrets of entrepreneurship. Many governments, nonprofit organizations, and institutions of higher learning have expressed their appreciation for my contributions to entrepreneurial ecosystems of the world.

You may submit conference requests to:
baltuntas@deulcom.com.tr.

# 15

## Follow my Lead

"A giving hand is always superior to one that takes."
**—Baybars Altuntas**

I have been very candid in telling you my life story. Have I missed anything? When I ask myself what I have done, the methods leading to my accomplishments can be boiled down to three steps: generate your business idea, get busy, and keep the ball rolling!

While I was a university student, I founded the Turkish Franchising Association for twenty-five cents. The association has now gathered under its umbrella nearly every franchise brand in Turkey. It generates hundreds of thousands of dollars of income through fairs, magazines, and publications every year. So what was my secret in founding this association? Very easy: while everyone else ignored it, I acted! Anyone could have done it, but they didn't. I wasn't in a better position to do it than anyone else. It just seemed logical to me, and figuring I had nothing to lose, I acted instead of sleeping on it.

While still a university student, I founded Deulcom with an investment of only $400 and made millions. So what was my secret? Very simple: to place an ad in a newspaper one Sunday, which anyone could have done, but they didn't.

Our prime minister had entrusted me with a letter to the US president, and President Obama had welcomed me in front of the world media as he proclaimed the importance of entrepreneurship in the twenty-first century. What was the secret to accomplishing this social venture? Very simple: the right business idea.

In the beginning, I had no money, no network, and no one to back me up. I did have good business ideas, however, and these came to me at the right time. I was an entrepreneur who could also keep the ball rolling.

So that's my life story in a nutshell. But I've missed something!

I may not be a very religious person, but I can easily see the writing on the wall when I look at the big picture. For that, I am grateful to God for all His support. He always answered my prayers.

As a result, I can assure you that you, too, can do what I did. You can become even more successful than I did. It is totally possible.

If you get stuck along the way, send me a message. Tell me what you started doing after reading this book. Follow me on Twitter, friend me on Facebook, join my website, follow my blogs. Always keep in touch.

I wish all the success in the world to all the future Baybars Altuntas entrepreneurs of tomorrow.

* * *

Don't forget: **Earn First, Spend Later.**
And follow me:
www.facebook.com/baybars.altuntas
www.twitter.com/baybarsaltuntas
www.youtube.com/baybarsaltuntas
www.baybarsaltuntas.com
www.baybarsaltuntasnotes.com
baltuntas@deulcom.com.tr

# A Toolkit for Entrepreneurs

Entrepreneurs need practical tips to set up their businesses. In this chapter, you will find eighty-one specific pieces of advice to help you get started. All these come from my own experiences.

**First, decide whether you are an entrepreneur or not.**

Take the first step to entrepreneurship by getting to know yourself. Aspiring to be an entrepreneur and actually becoming one are two very different things. Do not disregard others people's opinions when you are evaluating yourself. I always ask my conference participants the three questions listed below. Your answers to these will help lead the way to your becoming an entrepreneur. While you are surely tempted by the irresistible idea of being your own boss, remember that you are, at the same time, taking responsibility for those who are traveling with you on this journey.

1. As a child, did you ever overhear people saying, "This child is going to be a big businessman when he grows up" or "He will be very rich when he grows up"?
2. Do you really want to be more independent, make your own decisions, and earn more money?
3. Are you resistant to stress and pressure? Do you easily give up when things go wrong, or can you motivate yourself right away?

## Do you have the quirky character of an entrepreneur?

Never forget that if everybody became an entrepreneur, there would be seven billion entrepreneurs in the world and the whole system would collapse. Yet when you ask anyone if they would like to be an entrepreneur, the answer is always yes. Now think about the following statements. If you agree with them wholeheartedly, welcome aboard!

1. When I think of new business ideas, I start talking out loud to myself.
2. I really dislike authority, but I am comfortable being in a position of authority.
3. I am a very positive person and a very good communicator. I love meeting new people.
4. I have excellent sales ability. I think fast, implement fast.
5. I am not afraid of making mistakes. I learn a lot from my mistakes.
   If you share these ideas, we have a lot in common.

## Here are the first steps to take when your business idea arrives.

You have a new business idea. Here is what you need to do first.

1. Do some simple market research to get a sense if whether your idea will work or not. Ask friends, family, colleagues, and "the man on the street" their opinions to see if this idea will sell! Make sure you smell money.
2. If you conclude that your business idea will sell, now it is time to plan your business. I recommend www.businessplan.com for guidance in preparing a business plan.
3. While developing your business plan, include the things you can do in marketing and ways to implement sales.

4. Take note of how you are going to finance this business. Do you have your own capital? Will you borrow it from family and friends? Will you get bank loans? Will you be looking for an angel investor? Or, like me, will you sell first and then invest? Or will you combine it all into a single basket?

## Don't put all your eggs in one basket.

1. When entrepreneurs have a new business idea, they have a tendency to ignore everything else in the world. Okay, you can be an entrepreneur; that's fine. Let's assume you have the necessary financing. But remember, there is no guarantee that your business will succeed. Make sure you have enough to survive in case your venture does not succeed and you lose all your money.
2. I minimized my risk when creating my business by using my "first sell, and then spend" method from the very beginning. I could easily replace my initial investment of $400 by tutoring. Not all ventures may fit into my "first sell, then spend" method, however.
3. For ventures that do not fit, the formula I recommend is this: if you have the finances to support the business, then do it; otherwise, definitely stay away. Although I have enough capital now, I do not mind looking at businesses that are outside my formula of "first sell, then spend."

## Take reasonable risk.

The notion of a reasonable amount of risk varies from one entrepreneur to another. The risk a university student would take will be different than that of a family man. Even more important than financial risk is a sound business model. When you develop a good business model, when you ask the right questions and give the correct answers, you come out with a reasonable risk map. This map leads you to the decision on what you can endure within the limits of your reasonable risk. You can follow my lead and ask yourself the following questions:

1. How much would I lose? If I lose, what is the net loss?
2. If I risk this amount and I am not successful, how long will it take me to replace this amount?

If you can define what you might lose and how long it would take you to recoup it, you have calculated the reasonable amount of risk. You are on the right track.

## Be careful when you are generating your business idea.

1. If you have good sales skills but lack the financing to build your business, you can get into entrepreneurship by becoming a distributor for a company.
2. If you are more talented in human resources than sales, you can start by purchasing a franchise of a company—for example, a textile company—where you can operate in the background.
3. You are working at management level for a company. You are skilled in business plans and are actually a good businessperson. You may be considered less skilled in sales and human resources, but maybe you are good at team-building. You can be an entrepreneur who can build a good team.
4. Finally, if you have sales skills, you can build your business regardless, with little capital. If you are less skilled in sales, you can become a franchisee or distributor for a company and build your own business from there. But of course, these all require financing.

## Make sure you build your network.

You definitely have to like people-collecting. I may be one of the world's most successful people at that. My success has a lot to do with my personal connections. My entrepreneurs also can benefit from my networking as an angel investor, and this is, in itself, the most important capital that I can offer to partnering entrepreneurs, apart from financial capital. Here are the methods I follow:

1. Deal with all kinds of associations. Not only the ones you are interested in, but also communicate with a wide variety of people, attend receptions, and expand your network.
2. Take business cards from people you meet, number them, and save them on your computer. By all means, send an e-mail to the new contact within the first forty-eight hours expressing how pleased you are to have met them.
3. Networking should be a lifestyle. Do not even go to the bathroom without your business cards in your pocket!
4. Do not disregard Internet tools for expanding your network. You have to be on Facebook, LinkedIn, YouTube, and Twitter. Every day, you need to tweet at least twice. Follow me on Twitter @baybarsaltuntas.

## Identify your target market precisely.

You need to define your consumer profile when preparing your marketing plan. For example, let's say that you are going to propose an English language course. Who is your target demographic? Is it university students, elementary school students, or working adults? Are they graduate students preparing to earn their master's degree abroad, or are they preparing for state exams? You have to develop a different marketing strategy for each one of your products.

1. To a large extent, your market will determine what your marketing plan will look like.
2. Avoid meeting with an advertising agency until you determine what the needs of your market are.
3. The first thing you need to do once you have identified your market is to find the right slogan. It should be no longer than 3-4 words. The message should explain to the customers that you understand them, that you know their needs, and that you are able to meet their needs in an affordable way without compromising the quality of the product.

## Analyze your competitors carefully.

We have a saying in Turkey: "Let the steam follow you." This is important for the entrepreneur. The most important action at this stage is to understand whether or not your business idea will be successful. This requires analyzing your competitors' strengths as well as their weaknesses. The result of this analysis will tell you if you should get right on it or throw in the towel and seek other ventures. Most entrepreneurs underestimate the value of this step.

When I built Deulcom, there was no other business like it, so it was easy for me to progress past step one. I was only able to expand Deulcom as quickly as I did because other businesses were unable to figure out what I had done.

While analyzing your competition, the following points are of the utmost importance. Grab a pen and paper and start comparing your product with your competitors' according to the list below.

1. What's the difference between your product and theirs?
2. How much are they selling theirs for, and how much are you willing to sell yours for?
3. Which marketing channels are they using, and what results are they getting from each channel?

4. If your product or service is unique, you should be able to put this across to the consumer clearly. It is great if you are offering a better product for a better price! But be careful that your affordable alternative doesn't end up with a cheap product image. If your competitors are placing their ads on the bus stops, maybe you should place your ads inside the busses. You have to utilize the marketing channels your competitors are not using.

My advice to you is to find a patent bureau or a patent attorney registered in your country. It's important.

1. Trademarks and copyrights are completely different things, and you need to understand both. Trademarks are related to entrepreneurial activities, whereas copyrights are related to artistic or intellectual property (e.g., music, books, films).
2. For brand registration, you can upload your emblem and logo onto the Internet.
3. Remember to get and register your web address from the Internet. I suggest using www.register.com.

## Choose one of three alternatives while setting up your business.

Now you have your business idea, you have completed the previous steps, and it looks like your business idea will work. It's time to set up your business. Choose one of the three alternatives listed below:

1. Sole proprietorship
2. A limited liability company
3. A corporation

I recommend starting a limited liability company to new entrepreneurs. Sole proprietorship has issues when trying to institutionalize, and a corporation has too many burdensome procedures for a new business. A limited liability company can be built with only one person at a reasonable cost. It has the ability to carry your venture for years to come.

**Here are tips for quickly building your business:**

1. Use an accountant when you found your company. They can quickly handle all the procedures when building your business. All you need to do is sign the necessary papers.
2. Brief your accountants regarding the operating areas of your company so that they can prepare the main articulations for your company accordingly.
3. Check the Internet to see if there is another company using that name.
4. You can often find the documents you need to found your company on your city's chamber of commerce website.
5. The rent contract is an important document for founding your company.
6. Your accountant, who will also keep the books for your company, will organize the papers to found your company and usually will not charge an extra fee for that.

**Here are some tips to help you find your office:**

1. First of all, you need to establish whether your customers are coming to you or if you are going to them. The answer to that will help you avoid making unnecessary expenditures when renting and furnishing your office.

2. You must pay attention to the following points if the customer will be coming to your office:
   a. Your office should be easy to find.
   b. Parking should be easy.
   c. It should be easily accessible.
3. There should be space on the exterior of the building to hang your sign.
4. If you will be going to the customer, you needn't open an office in a visible or central location. You can rent an office at the most reasonable part of the city.
5. You need to add the following special conditions to your lease contract: "This lease may be terminated unilaterally by the tenant with a one-month notice. In this case, the tenant will not be responsible for any rent occurring after the tenant vacates the premises."

**Be aware of the following when you are signing your rental lease:**

1. If possible, ask for one month's rent free to cover the cost of repairs, depending upon the condition of the premise.
2. Determine where your sign will hang and specify the location in the rental contract.
3. Mention in the contract how many days of the week and at which hours the building will be open.
4. If your office or workplace requires a license with the municipality, mention in the contract that the landlord is required to supply you with all the necessary documents.
5. The deposit amount should not exceed the cost of two months' rent, or whatever is in line with the laws of your country, and mention this in the contract. If you can, pay the deposit with a bank check so as to retain your cash.

Do not forget these details when signing a rental contract. I have learned these to be very important from personal experience.

**Here are tips to remember when dealing with lawyers:**

1. You can have two types of contracts with a lawyer. You can hire a lawyer on a contractual basis and pay them on a monthly basis, or you can work with a lawyer that you pay on a case-by-case basis.
2. Bear in mind that if you pay monthly, years down the road, they could feasibly ask for severance pay if you decide to discontinue their services.
3. In some countries, if your company's capital is over a certain amount, you are required to retain a lawyer, and you are obligated to provide a copy of the contract to the chamber of commerce where you are registered. Whether you need a lawyer or not depends on what the law stipulates. If you are in the process of building your company, keep the capital under that line to avoid such an expense.
4. Unless you have a really intense legal process, it would make better sense to make a deal with a lawyer on a case-by-case basis.

## Please note the following when choosing your advertising agency.

After building your company, you will need external support from an accountant, a lawyer, and an advertising agency. Please take note of what I say below in choosing your advertising agency.

1. Make sure there are people with an entrepreneurial spirit within the advertising agency team. Only advertisers with the entrepreneurial spirit know that your prioritized destination as an entrepreneur is "sales."

2. I have been working with the same professional for about twenty years now. I change my advertising agency according to whatever agency she is in. She understands even from the tone of my voice which customer profile I am aiming for. Even though she is not an entrepreneur herself, with her entrepreneurial spirit, she knows best that I would rather have a selling ad than an artistic one. For this reason, I prepare advertising campaigns for my companies in cooperation with her and her team.
3. Explain in detail to the advertising agency that you are not after an artistic advertisement, but a selling one.

## Get your business card printed.

You may have noticed that, even as a student, I had business cards. If you intend to build your own business, immediately have business cards printed. There is no need for an address. I would be impressed if you were to hand me a business card with the following information:

- James Crown
- Entrepreneur
- Phone and e-mail

1. The cost of printing 1,000 business cards will not be a financial burden. Business cards will bring you to an equal level with the person you are doing business with. Instead of asking a businessman for his business card, it is a much better move to hand them your business card first and expect the same in return.
2. Have your business cards printed on a high-quality paper.
3. Choose a stylish design and a classy font. Let your card "smell" of business.

## Define your emblem and logo.

Start with your branding work as soon as the address of your company is defined. Talk to your advertisement agency and let them prepare an attractive businesslike logo and emblem for you.

1. Emblems and logos are very important. It is like naming your children. Make sure to get professional input.
2. As soon as your emblem and logo is defined, register your brand according to the patent laws in your country.
3. Prepare your corporate identity immediately.

When you set your emblem and logo, have your corporate identity set printed. This set, which will help you especially with corporate sales, consists of five basic items:

- envelopes large enough to fit a large-size file folder
- envelopes for small letters
- letterhead
- pocket folders
- Post-it notes

## Get your invoice and billing receipts printed.

Get your invoice and bill of sales receipts printed with your emblem and logos immediately. Legal requirements for these vary from country to country.

1. Your sales receipt should be in triplicate, perforated, and numbered. The first copy goes to your customer, the second to your accountant, and the third one stays with you.
2. You do not need permission from the revenue office to have receipts printed. These can be printed at any printing house.

3. You should also have your invoice sheets printed in triplicate. These should generally be printed at a printing house that is recognized by the revenue office, depending on the laws in your country. The printing house numbers the invoices and delivers them to you with a delivery record. Don't ever lose this delivery record. Put it in your company foundation file. The printing house will send a copy of it to your tax office. Losing your invoices is a major inconvenience, and it would be extremely hard to explain this to the revenue office. Check your invoice receipts closely every month.

## Get your signs ready.

1. Once your emblem and logo are ready, have your sign prepared for the exterior of your office building. Take a photo of the exterior of your building to give to your advertising agency.
2. Vinyl signs vary in cost according to size. It may cost up to $1,000 for a one hundred-square-meter office building in most areas.
3. If your office is in a zone with heavy traffic, it would be useful to have an illuminated sign. This can cost up to 50 percent more, but it will be worth it.

## Prepare for yourself a corporate articulation file.

Entrepreneurs can get a little distracted. I have seen entrepreneurs who have lost their most important official documents. Actually, I might have been like that in the very beginning, because there wasn't anyone to tell me how to do anything.

1. Get a file, and collect all your important documents in it, such as:
   - the main company contract,
   - the chamber of commerce registration,
   - signature circulars,
   - invoice delivery minutes,
   - bank accounts details,
   - the municipal license,
   - tax certificates,
   - the Social Security letter of notification,
   - the establishment minutes from the revenue office,
   - revenue office and Social Security system passwords,
   - equipment warranties, and so on.
2. Work with a bank that has a branch conveniently located near your place of business.
3. Do not get a POS credit card device unless you absolutely need it. Each POS device will cost only a small amount of money when it is inactive, but at the end of the year, without noticing it, you can easily accumulate hefty charges when you have multiple devices.

## Open a bank account.

Once you establish the company, you will need to open a bank account. I have quite a few pointers for you on this topic.

1. If you need a POS device, negotiate with your bank for an inactive POS limit. Some banks do not charge you if you have a minimum usage amount. The limits vary from bank to bank. Negotiate the terms of usage.
2. Since you may need to pay for a checkbook, think twice before you have one printed. (In the United States, check your options; many banks offer free business checking accounts.)

3. I recommend declining offers of automatic account credits from your bank account. These small automatic account loans differ between $5,000 and $20,000, and at the end of the year you will notice you have been charged a high interest rate for this kind of credit. Instead, let the bank call you when your balance goes below a certain limit so that you can make a deposit. Otherwise, you won't have any idea that you are being sold credit with the highest interest rates. I speak from experience!

4. Make sure you visit the bank manager and introduce yourself. Let him know what sort of a business plan you have, the nature of business model you have developed, and the revenue expectation you have for your company. Once every three months, make sure you visit him with reports about the development of your company. This will have a positive effect on your relationship.

5. Try to understand what you can do to help the bank create a new customer pool. You let the bank promote their products to your customers. Try killing two birds with one stone. Your customer will benefit from discounted services at the bank, which is a clear benefit for them, and your bank gets new customers. When you need new loan from the bank, you are in a position to ask for it, with the unspoken message that you have provided benefits to them that you didn't have to do, so it's their turn now to return the favor.

# Additional Resources

## Accelerators

www.sosventures.com

SOSventures is an accelerator VC, and runs a number of vertical accelerator programs around the world. Accelerators are a way to hasten the product/market fit of new ventures, to receive seed capital and mentoring, and to attract follow-on funding. SOSventures runs some of the world's leading accelerators for high tech entrepreneurs in software, hardware, biotech, media and food.

## Access to Finance in Latin America

www.reofcapital.com

Here you can find access to resources for technology entrepreneurs seeking angel investors, early stage venture capital and mid-market private equity funding in the United States (Southeast, Mid-Atlantic, Northeast, Mid-West and West Coast) and Latin America (Caribbean, Central America and Andean Region). This site also provides resources for entrepreneurs seeking capital, advice and research in other industries such as real estate, distressed assets and debt, energy, hospitality and healthcare, among others.

## Arabreneur

www.arabreneur.com

Arabreneur engages young entrepreneurs in the MENA region in their development and provides them with facilities to use their creativity and time to develop start-up companies that will lead to economic and social growth. You can follow the entrepreneurship eco-system in the MENA region as well as apply for Arabreneur's seed fund, acceleration, entrepreneurship events and training and find mentors in the MENA region. Arabreneur is the gateway for entrepreneurs to enter the MENA market.

## ArcticStartup

www.arcticstartup.com

ArcticStartup is an independent technology blog that reports on digital start-ups and growth entrepreneurship in the Nordic and Baltic countries.

## Balkan Venture Forum

www.balkanventureforum.org

The Balkan Venture Forum is the pioneer start-up and venture capital forum in South-East Europe, gathering the top innovation, knowledge and finance twice a year. Its website has details on upcoming forums, a blog with news about the community, and opportunities to apply for the various competitions organized within the forum.

## Baybars Altuntas Fan Club

www.baybarsaltuntasfanclub.com

Run by my fans, this is a club you can join for free to find photographs and videos about my adventures in entrepreneurship. You can also find the dates and venues for my conferences around the world.

## Baybars Altuntas Official Website

www.baybarsaltuntas.com

You can follow all my endeavors on this website. I continually update my blog with new entrepreneurial tips and other information. It is a great resource for the up-and-coming entrepreneur.

## Berkonomics

www.berkonomics.com

With a new posting each week and subscriptions by RSS or email, this blog by well-known angel investor and small business expert Dave Berkus gives important tips to entrepreneurs from starting up through growth and successful exit. A must-read for executives and entrepreneurs worldwide.

## BrainsClub

www.brainsclub.org

Founded by start-up grande dame Selma Prodanovic, BrainsClub is a dynamic community dedicated to enabling and empowering one million new entrepreneurs from around the world. BrainsClub members have access to first-class entrepreneurial experience and knowledge, unique personal development support, and conceivably the most influential and visionary entrepreneurs of our time. A single premium membership worth one million euro is available once a year.

## Danish Venture Capital and Private Equity

www.dvca.dk

DVCA is the trade association for a wide range of investors in Denmark and concentrates on making Denmark an even more attractive place to invest, both nationally and globally.

## Dave Berkus

www.berkus.com

Dave Berkus is a well-known angel investor and entrepreneur. On this site, he shares video excerpts from his keynote speeches, his TV segment entitled "The Berkus Report," and his TEDx talk on entrepreneurism. Dave covers stories of entrepreneurial successes and even failures, tips for entrepreneurs from Berkonomics, and more.

## Doing Business in Emerging Countries

www.bricandchina.com

BRIC expert, speaker, entrepreneur and thought leader, David Thomas is well known in the Asia Pacific region for his experience, credibility and passion for identifying, building and facilitating business and investment relationships between developed and emerging countries. In his blog you can follow his travels around the BRIC, MINT and other emerging countries and uncover new opportunities for business, investment and trade.

## Doing Business in Russia

www.ved.gov.ru/eng/

This website offers the latest information on the external trade of Russia, the rules you need to know when working in the Russian market, and the possibilities of doing business. It will also help to find partners for export, import or investment and to check their experience and reputation.

## Dragons' Den

www.ddturkiye.com – Turkey

http://abc.go.com/shows/shark-tank - USA

http://www.bbc.co.uk/dragonsden - UK

*Shark Tank* and *Dragons' Den* paved the way for aspiring entrepreneurs who want to start their own businesses by finding partners and financing opportunities. These sites are a great resource for learning pitching techniques.

## EBAN – European Business Angels Network

www.eban.org

EBAN represents the interests of business angels, business angel networks and federation networks, seed funds, and other entities involved in bridging the equity gap in Europe.

## EntreCity

http://entrecity.com/

The idea behind EntreCity is to help entrepreneurs build successful businesses by equipping entrepreneurs with tools and skills necessary for success. EntreCity presents online entrepreneurship courses and mentorship for aspiring entrepreneurs. Start courses to help acquire the right mind-set, EntreCity entrepreneur in developing a business plan and learning to funds.

## Entrepreneurship

www.entrepreneurship.org

This is a website where you can follow worldwide developments regarding entrepreneurship. It is an online community designed as a resource for entrepreneurs, policymakers, researchers, and academics around the world.

## ESTBAN – Estonian Business Angels Network

www.estban.ee

EstBAN is an umbrella organization for business angels and business angel groups seeking investment opportunities in Estonia and its neighboring regions with an aim to grow the quantity and quality of seed stage investments.

## European Tech

www.tech.eu

This website covers the European tech industry.

## Finding Investment for Your Entrepreneurial Project or Company

www.techtour.com

The Tech Tour is a platform and community for hi-tech entrepreneurs (from early to late stage), innovative investors, corporates and government influencers. The organization is committed to the development of emerging technology companies from Europe by bringing together the top entrepreneurial talent with European and International investors. The Tech Tour facilitates connections among key members of the innovation ecosystem and has been a launchpad for many successful hi-tech companies.

## Global Entrepreneurship Library

http://globalentrepreneurshiplibrary.org

The Global Entrepreneurship Library is an international portal of knowledge and resources to enable success with contributors and curators around the world. Resources can be filtered by topic, market, resource type and stage of business – from idea stage through to an exiting business.

## Global Entrepreneurship Research Network

http://gern.co

The Global Entrepreneurship Research Network is a working coalition of institutions dedicated to using research as a tool in realizing the full potential of entrepreneurship to create inclusive prosperity on a global scale. The site gives updates on the latest research from members such as the Kauffman Foundation, World Bank, Endeavor Insight and others.

## Global Entrepreneurship Congress

http://gec.co

The Global Entrepreneurship Congress is an inter-disciplinary gathering of start-up champions from around the world – where entrepreneurs, investors, researchers, thought leaders and policymakers work together to help bring ideas to life, drive economic growth and expand human welfare.

## Global Entrepreneurship Program

http://www.state.gov/e/eb/cba/entrepreneurship/gep/

GEP is a US State Department-led effort to promote and spur entrepreneurship by catalyzing and coordinating private-sector and US government programs to support entrepreneurs around the world.

## Global Entrepreneurship Week

http://gew.co

Millions of people participate in GEW events, activities and competitions every November. This site provides an overview of what is happening in the start-up ecosystems of 150 countries throughout the year and directs readers to in-depth information and resources designed to support entrepreneurs at the country level.

## Helping Businesses Expand Globally

www.globetrade.com

Global small business expert, speaker, entrepreneur and author Laurel Delaney is passionate about helping entrepreneurs and small businesses expand their businesses internationally. Her book, "Exporting: The Definitive Guide to Selling Abroad Profitably" is considered the bible on exporting and her global small business blog is ranked No. 1 in the world for entrepreneurs and small businesses interested in going global.

## LDJ Capital

www.ldjcapital.com

LDJ Capital is a family office with vast expertise in business development and substantial access to capital markets globally and a vast network of entrepreneurial and managerial relationships that provide its clients with world-class resources to drive growth, enhance brand exposure and add value. With decades of collective experience in advising, operating and investing in a wide range of businesses, they seek to partner with experienced management teams, leverage our network of contacts, and create sustainable sources of value for our clients and portfolio companies.

## Lean Disruptor

www.leandisruptor.com

This website is about Raomal Perera's journey in search of tools and processes to help companies with their growth strategies.

## Links Angel BAN

www.linksangelban.com

I created this website to help angel investors find new entrepreneurs with excellent business ideas. It is thus a place where angel investors and budding entrepreneurs can find each other.

## Migrant Woman Magazine

www.migrantwoman.com

This website provides high quality magazine content that is both for and about intelligent and aspirational migrant women with a positive mindset who have the determination and the drive to succeed in leading a happier life. Business and entrepreneurism are key features, including "Ask the Dragon". The overall purpose is to inspire and empower women of the universe. It is a platform for building a community of shared interests and vision, encouraging collaboration, ideas, vision and a shared understanding.

## Mr. All Biz and The Self-Employed

www.mrallbiz.com

www.theselfemployed.com

Senior small-business columnist at *USA Today* and author of fifteen books, including *The Small Business Bible*, Steven Strauss hosts entrepreneurs at both of these sites.

## Oasis 500

www.oasis500.com

Oasis 500 is a creative industries, technology, ICT, digital media and mobile sector business accelerator and investment company based in Amman, Jordan anchored by the King Abdullah II Fund for Development with regional and global reach. The first of its kind in Jordan and the MENA region, the company began with the concept of building a new platform for entrepreneurship by helping passionate, ambitious entrepreneurs start their own companies.

## Rainmaking

www.rainmaking.co.uk

Rainmaking is a "company factory" – they launch start-ups, build them into solid businesses, and eventually exit them. Today Rainmaking runs a portfolio of 15 companies with a total of 250 team members in their offices in Copenhagen, London and Berlin.

## SmallBizLady

www.succeedasyourownboss.com

This resource blog is published by Melinda Emerson, who is regarded as America's number one small-business expert. She publishes resources for start-up and existing entrepreneurs on business planning, management, marketing, and social media.

## Startup Nations

http://startupnations.org

Startup Nations is a network dedicated to identifying policy levers that can unleash high impact entrepreneurship and innovation. This site provides updates from member countries exploring different regulatory changes and other policy approaches while sharing ideas on what is working – and what isn't.

## Start-up Open

http://startupopen.com
Startup Open is a global competition to identify and recognize promising start-up companies founded within the last year. The site enables you to learn more and enter the competition with prizes including a trip to the Global Entrepreneurship Congress, mentoring experiences and more.

## Startupbootcamp

www.startupbootcamp.org
Originally launched in Copenhagen, Startupbootcamp is a global network of industry-focused start-up accelerators. We take start-ups global by giving them direct access to an international network of the most relevant partners, investors and mentors in their sector.

## Startups in Central and Eastern Europe

www.goaleurope.com
On this website you can find news about software development, outsourcing and investments in high-tech industries in Russia, Central and Eastern Europe.

## SuperFounders

www.superfounders.com
SuperFounders is a start-up acceleration and investment platform for South-East Europe. It supports and develops a start-up community across many cities from the region, providing its acceleration programs and events. Its website is a repository of start-up resources, news blogs, calendar of events and programs, including the opportunity to apply for them.

## Tenmou

www.tenmou.me
Tenmou is a Bahrain-based angel investment group. Their website is a good resource to learn about angel investments in the Middle East, as

well as posts from angel investors talking about what they are looking for in their investments.

## The Ewing Marion Kauffman Foundation
www.kauffman.org
This center is located in Kansas City, Missouri, USA and is number one in the world in educating entrepreneurs towards building their own businesses. It is also often referred to as the world's largest foundation devoted to entrepreneurship.

## The Soho Loft Media Group
www.thesoholoft.com
The Soho Loft Media Group is a global financial media company with 3 divisions: *Times Impact Publications* produces relevant content on investing and entrepreneurship that is published and syndicated in a growing list of over 100 leading online publications. *The Soho Loft Conferences* organizes up to 200 investor-focused global summits, talks and events annually. *Victoria Global* Corporate Communications specializes in client Investor Relations, Public Relations, Branding and Social Media Marketing.

## Times Reality News
www.timesrealtynews.com
Times Realty News is a media stream for the emerging real estate crowdfunding industry. TRN is at the forefront of this exciting phenomenon because of the changing landscape in realty financing made possible through the JOBS Act (Jumpstart Our Business Startups Act) and other new and alternative trends in financing. It chronicles the work and growth of the real estate crowdfunding platforms, entrepreneurs, developers, investors, professionals, experts, technologists, innovators, media and educators in this industry.

## VentureBeat
www.venturebeat.com
This is a leading source for news and perspective on technology innovation. News, analysis, and events provide deep context to help executives, entrepreneurs, and tech enthusiasts make smart decisions.

## VentureConnect

www.ventureconnect.ro

Established in Bucharest, Romania, the VentureConnect Foundation is the most active matchmaking platform between technology entrepreneurs and appropriate early-stage investors in the SEE –South-East Europe region. Entrepreneurs can apply for their projects, run for the pitching sessions, meet with investors in real-life forums and find a lot of other useful entrepreneurship resources within the web page.

## Victoria Global

www.victoriaglobal.co

Victoria Global is your Corporate Communications partner focused on giving your company a voice. With their history of financial innovation, expertise and network in both institutional investing and crowd financing, they offer an integrated approach to create cutting-edge public, investor and social media relations for your company by using balanced and multi-tiered systems and strategies. As the voice of your company, Victoria Global connects you with your crowd and audience.

## WBAA – World Business Angels Association

www.wbaa.biz

The World Business Angels Association is the official website for all angel investors throughout the world. Their mission is to stimulate communication on business practices in the field of angel capital financing.

## WEBIT Congress

www.webitcongress.com

Every year over 10,000 participants from 110 countries attend the Global Webit Congress, which bridges Europe, the Middle East, Africa and Asia. It is a global event for digital, tech and telco industries that supports the growth of the digital and tech industry, and promotes knowledge and know-how to create the best possible business networking event. Featured attendees and speakers are top executives from Apple, PayPal, Google, Facebook, Yahoo!, Unilever, Stripe, Seamless, Ubuntu, Coursera, Nissan, Amazon, IBM, Yandex, Qualcomm, Cisco, Akamai and many more.

## WFC –World Franchise Council

http://www.worldfranchisecouncil.net/

The WFC is the global organization of franchise associations supporting the development and protection of franchising and promoting a collective understanding of best practices in fair and ethical franchising worldwide.

## World Entrepreneurship Forum

www.world-entrepreneurship-forum.org

The World Entrepreneurship Forum, based in France, brings together entrepreneurs from all over the world under the same umbrella. It was created in 2008 with one main belief: in front of the current main disruptive changes the world is facing, entrepreneurship, by creating both wealth and social justice, is key to shaping the world of 2050.

## Xevin

www.xevin.eu

Xevin is the website of most active VC in Central and Eastern Europe.

# References

[1] "Remarks by the President at Cairo University, 6-04-09." The White House. June 4, 2009. Accessed August 24, 2014. http://www.whitehouse.gov/the_press_office/Remarks-by-the-President-at-Cairo-University-6-04-09.

[2] "Remarks by the President at the Presidential Summit on Entrepreneurship." April 26, 2010. Accessed August 24, 2014. http://www.whitehouse.gov/the-press-office/remarks-president-presidential-summit-entrepreneurship.

[3] "Edirne." Travel Guide at Wikivoyage. Accessed August 24, 2014. http://en.wikivoyage.org/wiki/Edirne.

[4] "Hazelnut." Wikipedia. Accessed August 24, 2014. http://en.wikipedia.org/wiki/Hazelnut.

[5] "Giresun." Travel Guide at Wikivoyage. Accessed August 24, 2014. http://en.wikivoyage.org/wiki/Giresun.

[6] "Tükiye'nin En Çok Istenen Şirketleri (Turkey's Most Desirable Companies to Work For)." Kariyer.NET, February 1, 2004.

[7] Bilesim Advertisement Index, January-May (1997).

[8] "Türkiye'nin Franchising Devleri 100 (Turkey's Top 100 Franchising Giants)." Ekonomist, September 8, 2013.

[9] Amorós, José Ernesto, and Niels Bosma. "Global Entrepreneurship Monitor Global Report 2013." Global Entrepreneurship Monitor. January 20, 2014. Accessed August 24, 2014. http://www.gemconsortium.org/docs/download/3106.

[10] Sohl, Jeffry. "The Angel Investor Market in 2007: Mixed Signs of Growth." University of New Hampshire. January 1, 2007. Accessed August 24, 2014. http://www.unh.edu/news/docs/2007AngelMarketAnalysis.pdf.

[11] "2014 ACA Summit." ACA Summit / Angel Capital Association. Accessed August 24, 2014. http://www.angelcapitalassociation.org/2014summit/.

[12] "€5.1 Billion Market Shows European Angels on the Rise!" EBAN (European Trade Association for Business Angels, Seed Funds and Early Stage Market Players). July 5,

2103. Accessed August 24, 2014. http://www.eban.org/e5-1-billion-market-shows-european-angels-on-the-rise/#.U_mADrySySJ.

[13] The World Bank and Ewing Marion Kauffman Foundation, "Identifying deals and investing" in Creating Your Own Angel Investor Group: A Guide for Emerging and Frontier Markets, (Washington, DC: World Bank, 2013), 54.

[14] "Tükiye'nin En Çok Istenen Şirketleri (Turkey's Most Desirable Companies to Work For)." *Kariyer.NET*, February 1, 2004.

[15] "Yerli Girişimcinin Kitabı Steve Jobs'u Solladı (Local Entrepreneur's Book Outsells Steve Jobs' Book)." Hürriyet. November 26, 2011. Accessed August 24, 2014. http://www.hurriyet.com.tr/ekonomi/19331522.asp.

[16] Aytaç, Gökmen. "Manisa'dan Baybars Altuntaş Geçti (Baybars Altuntaş Pays a Visit in Manisa)." Milliyet. November 20, 2011. Accessed August 24, 2014. http://www.milliyet.com.tr/manisa-dan-baybars-altuntas-gecti/gokmen-aytac/ege/yazardetay/22.11.2011/1465783/default.htm.

# About the Author

**Baybars Altuntas is a serial** entrepreneur, angel investor, and leader of many global social responsibility projects. He was recognized by The European Trade Association of Business Angels as the 2013's Best Individual in Europe Globally Engaging with Entrepreneurial Ecosystem. He was the only entrepreneurial guru to be granted a personal audience with President Obama at the Presidential Summit on Entrepreneurship in Washington, DC, which was hailed by the White House as the most important entrepreneurial event of the twenty-first century. In his meeting with President Obama, he shared his ideas on how to convert public money to smart money globally and to ease entrepreneurs' access to finance.

He is now a global leader in entrepreneurship and shows the way for new generations to become successful with his unique system known as "The map to success: Your rise to entrepreneurship®." His books have been translated into several languages and have become bestsellers in each of them. Altuntas has addressed more than one hundred thousand entrepreneurs of all ages worldwide, each of them attending his conferences seeking the knowledge required to succeed in life. When Altuntas was still a university student, he was recognized as one of the forty most innovative businessmen of Turkey. His life story was made into a film by TRT, the official broadcasting service of Turkey. Altuntas is the pioneer of the franchising system in Turkey and the Balkan countries. He is also known as the father of franchising in Turkey. He is the founder of the Turkish Franchising Association, which represents Turkey at the World Franchise Council. His best-selling book set a record for twenty-four reprints within the first six months of publication and even outsold Steve Jobs' book. Altuntas has inspired thousands of people with his words of encouragement: "I did it my way, then you can too!" He is a respected visionary who provides consulting to CEOs and Forbes 1000 businessmen in addition to writing books and making speeches. He is a global expert in wannapreneurship, entrepreneurship, innovation, marketing and sales, branding, institutionalization, franchising, leadership, and angel investment. Altuntas is one of the one hundred Dragons who have appeared on the world-famous angel investment and entrepreneurship TV show, Dragons' Den. The program is well-known in the USA as Shark Tank.

As an angel investor, he has invested in numerous start-up companies. He is the president of the Business Angels Association of Turkey (TBAA), and Vice President of the European Trade Association for Business Angels, Seed Funds, and other Early Stage Market Players (EBAN), which represents seventy-five thousand business angels in Europe.

He also leads the biggest business angel network in Turkey: Links Angel BAN. His "The map to success: Your rise to entrepreneurship®" system guarantees success in everyday life for people of all ages. In his conferences, workshops, and seminars, he describes nine different paths. When you connect all nine, you begin to see the true story that brought Altuntas his own success. These nine paths comprise the basic principles of entrepreneurship that he describes in his books and conferences. More than one hundred thousand people from around the world have found new inspiration from his conferences. He is profiled regularly on leading international media such as CNN International, Bloomberg, and NTV, among others. He is a co- author of Planet Entrepreneur: The World Entrepreneurship Forum's Guide to Business Success Around the World, published by Wiley in November 2013.

The technique of converting idle capacity into cash has been examined by academicians and referred to in international management journals as the Altuntas Principle. This highlights the fact that there is no need for finance if you are a great entrepreneur. This concept has inspired many entrepreneurs who had been unable access to finance, but who had a great idea and the ability to develop the correct business model and implement it.

He is the Ambassador of the World Entrepreneurship Forum to the Balkans and Turkey. He earned his bachelor's degree from Bosphorus University in Turkey. He is married and has two daughters.

www.baybarsaltuntas.com